FAITH IN GOD
AND
FULL SPEED AHEAD!

FE EN DIOS
Y ¡ADELANTE!

FAITH IN GOD
AND
FULL SPEED AHEAD

FE EN DIOS Y ¡ADELANTE!

Dichos from the Trucks and Buses
of
Mexico and Latin America

Collected and Edited by
GRANT LA FARGE
with text translations by
Bernadette Rodríguez

Sunstone Press
Santa Fe, New Mexico

FIRST EDITION
Photographic Illustrations by Grant La Farge

Printed in the United States of America

Library of Congress Cataloging in Publication Data

La Farge, Grant, 1928 –
Faith in God – and full speed ahead!
Fé in Diós – y ¡adelante!
Sayings on trucks and buses in Mexico and Latin America.

Bilingual: English and Spanish
Bibliography, p.
1. Epigrams. I. Title. II. Title: Fe en Dios y Adelante!
PN6285.L33   1985   080'.9'8   84–23948
ISBN: 0-86534-050-1

Published in 1985 by SUNSTONE PRESS
Post Office Box 2321 / Santa Fe, New Mexico 87504-2321 / USA

TABLE OF CONTENTS
TABLE DE MATÉRIAS

For
Patricia Arscott La Farge
her love for the Folk Art of the Latin Americas
and for the spirit of their peoples
has been my inspiration and the inspiration for
Faith in God - Full Speed Ahead

para
Patricia La Farge Arscott
por su amor por el Arte Folklórico de América Latina
y por el espíritu de su gente
fué mi inspiración y la inspiración de
Fé En Diós - y ¡ Adelante!

PROLOGO

Oaxaca: *Si Sufres con El Vente con Migo. If You Suffer with Him, Come with Me!*
Large Farm Truck

NOTE: The following abbreviations have been used throughout the book for types of vehicles with dichos on them:

NOTA: Las siguientes abreviaciones aparecen en el libro y indican los tipos de vehículos que tienen dichos:

22-T	= 22-wheel transport	=	camión - 22 ruedas
18-T	= 18-wheel transport	=	camión - 18 ruedas
LFT	= large farm truck	=	camión - 10 ruedas
MFT	= medium farm truck	=	camión - 6 ruedas
SFT	= small farm truck	=	camión - 4 ruedas
PT	= pickup truck	=	camión - "pickup"
DT	= dump truck	=	camión - volquete
TT	= tank truck	=	camión de petróleo
M-Bus	= microbus	=	micro-autobus
F, B, S	= front, back, side	=	delante, detrás, lado

This is a book about people. about humor, and about the expression of passionate feelings on vehicles of many kinds.

In the United States of America, we use bumper stickers for communication and for amusement. Topics cover a broad spectrum of interest, as exemplified by:

Religion:	***Honk if you love Jesus!***
Politics:	***Don't blame me, I didn't elect him!***
Wit:	***This is not a bumper sticker, it's a flat banana!***
Philosophy:	***A Mind is like a parachute - it only functions when its open***
Double meaning:	***Dangerous curves ahead***
Nonsense:	$E = MC^2 \pm 1\ db$

Bumper stickers are succinct: they speak out on behalf of the driver of a car or, sometimes, a truck, (rarely a bus), and are addressed to any who will note and enjoy them — *...Make Better Lovers* —or who even may be willing to respond — *Honk if you love...* — Often, they are very clever and very funny, sometimes informative, occasionally banal. Bumper stickers are the principal medium of North American automotive expression.

In Mexico and the Latin Americas, small printed decals sometimes are seen on vehicles, but virtually never on the bumper; bumper stickers are extremely rare. This rarity reflects international, philosophical differences. The people of the United States lean toward technology. They prefer to design clever sayings, statements or advertisements — some with illustrations — and to have them printed by a commercial press in several colors on self-sticking plastic paper. It is then only necessary to procure and to apply them. Even the procurement may be made easy by an organization which sends a bumper sticker as a membership benefit. Although satisfying to the need for instant gratification, what is missing in this production and application is our selves: our intimate, personal involvement.

The Latin American loves, characteristically, to be in the midst of whatever is going on, doing and being, encouraging and maintaining a close relationship with the people and objects in the surrounding world. Our northern sense of privacy contrasts with the strong Latin need to communicate personally and intimately to and with other members of a naturally sociable species. The vehicular expressions of this need are *dichos* — my wife defines them as "informal, personal 'position' papers" — and they are the subject of this book. *Dichos* are appealing for the very reason that what they express *is* so personal. Virtually all are painted by hand: sometimes simply, in only one color; sometimes ornately and in several colors. Some are in handwriting, some in labored Gothic script; occasionally, *Dichos* are illustrated with simple, or florid paintings. Whether they are painted crudely or ornately, it is always, always accomplished with passion.

The history of the *dicho* is a long and illustrious one, and it is reviewed in an entertaining collection of Inscripciones — or *dichos* — from Argentina, by Norberto Folino entitled:

Este libro es tocante al humor, a la gente, y sobre la expresión de la sensibilidad apasionada sobre vehículos de muchas clases.

En los Estados Unidos de América, usamos bumper stickers para comunicar y para la diversión. Los temas cubren amplias ideas de interés, ejemplificadas por:

La Religión:	*¡Piten si aman a Jesús!*
La Política:	*¡No me hechen la culpa a me, yo no lo elegí!*
El Humór:	*¡Esto no es un bumper sticker, es un platano aplastado!*
La Filosofía:	*¡El Entendimiento es como un paracaídas—solo funciona cuando está abierto!*
Lo Absurdo:	$E = MC^2 \pm 1\ db$

Bumper stickers son breves: hablan a favor del chofer de un coche, o a veces de un camión (raramente de un autobus), y son dirigidos a cualquier persona que los note y que los goce — *...Hacen Mejores Amantes* — o que tal vez quieran contestar — *Piten Si Aman a ...*—. Frecuentemente, son muy habiles y muy chistosos, a veces informativos, ocasionalmente banál. En Norte América, bumper stickers son el medio principal de la expresión automotriz.

En México y en América Latina, a veces se ven etiquetas engomadas (rótulos) en los vehículos, pero virtualmente nunca se ven sobre el contrachoque. Bumper stickers son muy raros. Esta raridad refleja diferencias internacionales y filosóficas entre los Estados Unidos y entre México y América Latina. La gente de Los Estados Unidos se inclina hacía la tecnología. Prefieren inventar dichos avisos, declaraciones, o advertencias — algunas con ilustraciones — y luego la prensa comerciale toma estas ideas y las imprimen sobre papel de plástico engomado. Entonces sólo es necesario conseguirlos y aplicarlos. A veces hasta se hace fácil conseguirlos porque algunas organizaciones mandan bumper stickers como parte de una ventaja por ser miembro. Aunque esto satisface la necesidad para la gratificación instante, lo que falta en esta producción y en la aplicación de estos bumper stickers es nuestro ser íntimo y toque personal.

Al Latino Americano le encanta, característicamente, estar en el rigor de cualquier cosa que está pasando, sea haciendo algo o sólo estando allí, pero siempre estimulando y manteniendo una relación unida con la gente y los objetos en el mundo alrededor. Nuestro sentido retirado contrasta con la necesidad que tiene el latino de comunicar personalmente y íntimamente con otros miembros de su própio especie sociable. Las expresiones vehículares de esta necesidad son dichos — mi esposa los describe como " 'papeles' personales y informales sobre posición" — y el propósito de este libro. Dichos son atraídos por la verdadera razón de los que expresan es tan personal. Virtualmente todos son pintados a mano: a veces sencillamente, en un sólo color; y a veces floridos y en muchos colores. Algunos estan escritos de su "puño y letra," algunos en escritura Gótica laborada. Ocasionalmente los dichos son ilustrados con pinturas sencillas o floridas. Sea pintados crudamente or ornadamente, siempre, siempre estan cumplidos con pasión.

*Chofer Buena Banana Busca Chica Buena Mandarina. Trucker Good-Banana
Seeks Cutie Good-Tangerine, or, Horny Trucker Seeks Buxom Cutie.*
(For this and other books listed below see Bibliography.)

Folino documents the appearance of contemporaneous decorative motifs on pre-
Christian sarcophagi and on Roman buildings. Later, both pictures and phrases
appeared on Sicilian donkey-carts, where they are seen in abundance to this very
day. Folino also presents a photograph taken July 11, 1909 (page 31, Folino's
book), of a *dicho* from a horse-drawn cart carrying produce in Argentina:

> *Soy y Sido y Seré / I am and I have been and I will be.*

A number of articles and books have been written about the adaptation of the
dicho to motor-driven vehicles. One of the earliest, from 1956, is by Arthur Woodward: *Names On Wheels.* The first edition of the popular Mexican book, *Picardía
Mexicana #*, by Jiménez, appeared in 1958, and was in its 69th printing by 1981!
His short chapter on Letreros en Camiones — Legends on Trucks — illustrates
about 50 *dichos* and includes their original crude lettering, misspellings and
coarse flavor!

Other articles on vehicular *dichos* have appeared subsequently:
• *The Mexican Truck Driver,* by Munro Edmonson in 1959;
• *The People's Guide to Mexico,* by Carl Franz in 1972;
• *Cawboy de Medianoche,* by James Jaquith in 1975;
• *Dichos, Dicharachos y Refranes Mexicanos,* by Editores Mexicanos Unidos in
   1977; and
• *Soul of the Mexican Trucker,* by Gloria Giffords in 1981.
Marilee Schmit selected the *dichos* of Ecuador as the subject of a thesis written
recently for the Department of Anthropology, University of New Mexico. Since
many dictionaries have proven helpful in the translation of *dichos*, especially
those with an emphasis on national and regional *modismos/idioms*, proverbs or
caló/slang, a list of these has been included in the bibliography.

One of the most interesting of the articles cited above is James Jaquith's statistical
analysis of Mexican *dichos* which appeared in *The New Scholar* in 1975. Its
strength lies in its classification of 905 *dichos* into 50 different thematic groups,
some dominant, like religion and love, some more scarce, like show business.
The weakness of Jacquith's analysis is shared with this book: only a fraction of
the total number of drivers could be interviewed; so many were either on the
highway, or away from their parked vehicles. The responses of the many I did in-
terview, some in dangerous and difficult circumstances, were uniformly positive
and encouraging: they took great joy in telling me all about their *dichos*.

The Latin American nomenclature for vehicular inscriptions varies: in most
countries, they are called *dichos* or sayings; in Peru, *creéncias/beliefs*; in Guatemala, either *dichos* or *refránes/proverbs*. There are literally tens of thousands of

La historia del dicho es larga e ilustre y está repasada en una colección entretenida de inscripciones — o dichos — de Argentina, escrita por Norberto Folino, entitulada:

> *Chofer Buena Banana Busca Chica Buena Mandarina,*
> or Camionero descalentado busca moza retozona atractiva.
> (Hay una bibliografia al cabo de este libro.)

Folino documenta la primera presentación de temas decorativos contemporáneos sobre sarcófagos pre-cristianos y sobre edificios Romanos. Despúes, se añadieron frases a las pinturas sobre los carretos sicilianos donde hasta hoy en día se ven en abundancia. Folino también presenta una fotografía, tomada el día 11 Julio 1909 (pagina 31, el libro de Folino), de un dicho sobre una carreta de caballo llevando verduras en Argentina:

> *Soy y Sido y Seré*

Una cantidad de artículos y libros se han escrito sobre la adaptación del dicho sobre vehículos motorizados. Uno de los más avanzados, de 1956, fué escrito por Arthur Woodward: *Names On Wheels.* La primera edición del libro Mexicano populár *Picardía Mexicana,* escrito por Jiménez, apareció en 1958, y para el año 1981 ya lo habían imprimido 69 veces! Su capítulo breve sobre *Letreros en Camiones* ilustra como 50 dichos e incluye el letrero original crudo, y la ortografía incorrecta y el sabor tosco!

Otros artículos sobre dichos vehiculares han aparecido subsecuentemente:
• *The Mexican Truck Driver,* escrito por Munro Edmonson en 1959;
• *The People's Guide to Mexico,* por Carl Franz en 1972;
• *Cawboy de Medianoche,* por James Jaquith en 1975;
• *Dichos, Dicharachos y Refranes Mexicanos,* por Editores Mexicanos Unidos en 1977; and
• *Soul of the Mexican Trucker,* por Gloria Giffords en 1981.
Marilee Schmit selección dichos del Ecuador como el sujeto para su tesis que escribió recentemente para el departamento de Antropolgía en la Universidad de Nuevo México. Ya que muchos diccionarios han sido útiles en el entendimiento de dichos especialmente esos con énfasis en modismos nacionales y regionales, o escritos en caló, una lista de estos diccionarios esta incluída en la bibliografía.

Uno de los artículos más interesantes mencionado antes es el análisis estadístico de dichos mexicanos de James Jaquith que apareció en *The New Scholar* en 1975. Su esfuerza esta pendiente en la clasificación de 905 dichos en 50 grupos tematicos, algunos dominantes como la religión y el amor, algunos más raros, como espectáculos públicos. La debilidad del análisis de Jaquith esta compartida con este libro: sólo parte del número de choferes se pudieron entrevistar. Muchos estaban viajando en la carretera o no estaban con sus vehículos estacionados. Las respuestas de muchos que sí pude entrevistar, algunos en circunstancias peligrosas o difíciles, fueron igualmente positivas y estimulantes. Todos tomaron mucho gusto hablándome de sus dichos.

trucks and buses with *dichos* painted on their bumpers, frames, hoods, cabs, windows, fuel tanks, and mud-flaps…in fact, almost anywhere there is room for a word or a sentence. *Dichos* appear on all ages and sizes of trucks from pickup trucks to 22-wheelers, on a very few private cars and taxis, on hand-carts and on all kinds of buses, though rarely on the first class Greyhound variety. The vehicles of nationalized companies and of the government rarely have *dichos.* Perhaps this is because the very processes of nationalization and urbanization are dehumanizing. Or is it because, as my Ecuadorian friend Hugo Herrera says, "In a country village, there is no censure"?

The purpose of this book is to present a collection of vehicular *dichos.* I hope they will provide a glimpse into another side of the passionate and involved spirit of the eight Latin American countries included. Moreover, I hope to entertain the reader, and to provide a bibliography for further perusal or study of this remarkable folk art. The title of the book, to use a Latin reflexive 'suggested itself' very readily, for it is by far the most common *dicho* in all countries visited:

Fé en Diós – y Adelante!
Have Faith in God – and Full Speed Ahead!

This is a clear statement of the two most important guiding forces on the Latin American highway. The first is the intense faith of the driver in the protection of God and His saints. The second is the absolutely "devil-may-care," almost suicidal, passionate recklessness with which almost all drivers approach vehicular travel "South of the Border."

Although, like Jaquith, I have arranged the *dichos* into chapters which encompass their principal subject or mood, there are many which may belong in more than one category. They embrace more than one subject or may have different meanings, rarely in the absence of an intent to create confusion. Those which clearly have double — or more — meanings are in a chapter by themselves. In all fairness, every *dicho* is at least double in meaning, for it is both the vehicle and the driver which speak. Thus, quite a few *dichos* have meanings on several levels and they enjoy the humor inherent in ambiguity!

Dichos appear on vehicles in many forms and with many flavors. Perhaps the most important and internationally pervasive subject is religion. Such *dichos* often take the form of invocations to God or to saints for protection and guidance on the highway, for the driver and for the vehicle:

Diós Bendiga Mi Camino / God Blesses My Way

or,   *Diós Bendiga Este Bus / God Bless This Bus*

Another large category includes messages of love, which may be serious, or frankly humorous:

Quiéreme Siempre / Love Me Always
TBC y TDG (Te Besé y Te Dejé) / I Kissed You and I Left You

La nomenclatura para las inscripciones vehículares latino -américanas es
variable: en la mayor parte de los países, se llaman dichos; en Perú, *creéncias*; en
Guatemala, *dichos o refranes*. Hay literalmente miles de camiones y autobuses
con dichos pintados sobre el contrachoque, el armazón, el capó, la cabina, las
ventanas, el tanque, y los guardabarros; casí en cualquier lugar que tenga espacio
para una palabra o una declaración. Dichos aparecen en todos años y tamaños de
camiones, de camiones pickup a camiones de 22 ruedas. Se ven en algunos
coches privados o en taxis, en carretas, y sobre todas clases de autobuses de
primera clase, como tipo Greyhound. Los vehículos de compañias na-
cionalizadas o que pertenecen al gobierno raramente tienen dichos. Quizás esto
será porque el verdadero proceso de la nacionalización y la urbanización es
deshumanizante, o tal vez será, como dice mi amigo ecuatoriano, Hugo Herrera,
"En los pueblitos no hay censura."

La intención de este libro es para presentar una colección de dichos vehículares.
Ojalá que provean un reflejo hacia el interior del espíritu apasionado y envuelto
de los ocho países latino-americanos incluídos. Además, espero entretener al
lector, y proveer una bibliografía para promover el estudio de este arte folklórico
tan notable. El título del libro, para usar el reflexivo, "se sugiró sólo" muy rapido,
porque es el dicho más comun en todos los países visitados:

Fé en Diós - y ¡Adelante!

Esta es una declaración clara de las dos fuerzas más importantes que guían las
carreteras latino-americanas. La primera es la fé intensa que tiene el chofer en
Diós y sus santos para protegerlo. La segunda es la actitud, sin reserva, casi
ruinosa a sus propios intereses, de la manera descuidada apasionada en que casi
todos los choferes manejan sobre las carreteras al sur de la frontera.

Aúnque, como Jaquith, he arreglado los dichos en capítulos que incluyen su sujeto o genio principal, hay muchos que pueden ser de otra categoría. Contienen
más de un sujeto o tienen más de un sentido, raramente en la ausencia del intento
para crear confusión. Los que claramente tienen más que un sentido están en un
capítulo aparte. En toda equidad, cada dicho es a lo menos doble en sentido, porque es los dos, el chofer y el vehículo que se expresan. Así es que muchos de los
dichos tienen sentidos sobre muchos niveles y gozan del humor intrínsico en ambigüedad!

Dichos aparecen sobre vehículos de muchos modelos y con muchos sabores. Tal
vez el sujeto más importante y el que aparece más internacionalmente es el de la
religión. Frecuentemente, tales dichos toman la forma de invocaciones a Diós o
los santos para la protección y dirección en la carretera, para el chofer y el
vehículo:

Diós Bendiga Mi Camino
y, *Diós Bendiga Este Bus*

Otra categoría grande incluye mensajes de amor, que pueden ser serios o francamente chistosos:

Sometimes *dichos* are double (or more) in meaning:

Guárdemelo, Virgencita / Keep it (him) for me, little Virgin

Proper names appear very frequently, most often in conjunction with other *dichos*, and almost always honoring the driver, his sweetheart, members of his family or friends; or the *dicho* may be just a nickname, or a humorous name, or the name of the vehicle and its company:

*Javiercito / Little Javier or Coadília or *Chinita or*
*Que **F**elicidad Es **O**rer y **R**esar a **D**iós;*
Martha Lys — Dulce Ma. — Leonel Gerardo or Pancho or Gargantua
and Brisas de las Cumbres - La Cumbreña /
Breezes of the Hills - The Hilly One Bus Line.

A chapter is devoted to humor: whimsy, jokes, signs, plays on words and blatant machismo or egotism:

El Pié Grande / Big Foot;
or   Se Solicita - El Consiente / We are soliciting - Someone of Sound Mind
or El Azúl Lado / On the Blue Side
or Diós Mi Diente (Adiós Mi Diente) / May God Keep My Tooth!
and   Estoy Muy Linda, Visitame / I'm very Beautiful, Visit Me

Dichos, thus, strongly proclaim the feelings of the owner or driver about many different aspects of an encompassing world. Another large category includes animals, birds, spirits and cartoon characters:

Búfalo Rojo / Red Buffalo; or Pato-Cito / Little Duck;
or El Duende / The Hobgoblin; and Papa Pitufo / Papa Smurf.

Occasionally, a trucker will paint as many as a half dozen different *dichos* on his vehicle; the record is sixteen on two Panamanian trucks owned by the same enthusiast! Street slang is used frequently. Misspellings and backward letters are very common. A few *dichos* are simply not translatable by a casual observer — only the driver-artist knows what is meant.

I have tried to use a consistent format throughout this book. Each chapter is divided into sections by country and by city or town nearest to where the *dicho* was seen and recorded. The *dicho* appears first in its original form, almost always in Spanish, exactly as it appeared on the vehicle, though without the backward letters. The original misspellings and aberrant capitalizations have been preserved. Sometimes they are, by themselves, entertaining or introduce ambiguity:

Estando Bien con Diós Me Vio [Fio] de los Habladores
Being 'in good' with God, I can Recognize (Am Free of] the Gossipers.

Quiéreme Siempre
y, *TBC y TDG (Te Besé y Te Dejé)*

A veces, dichos son de doble — o más — sentidos:

Guárdemelo, Virgencita

Nombres propios aparecen muy frecuentamente, muchas veces en unión con
otro dichos, y casi siempre honrando al chofer, su enamorada, miembros de sus
familias o amigos. También, los dichos puede ser un apodo o nombre placentero,
o es nada más que el nombre del vehículo y de la compañía:

Javiercito / o Coadília o   Chinita o
*Que **F**elicidad **E**s **O**rer y **R**esar a **D**iós*
Martha Lys - Dulce Ma. - Leonel Gerardo / o Pancho o Gargantua;
y, Brisas de las Cumbres - La Cumbreña

Un capítulo está dedicado al humor, al chiste, al suspiro, juegos en palabras, y el
machismo o egoísmo:

El Pié Grande
o, Se Solicita - El Consiente
o, El Azúl Lado
o, Diós Mi Diente (Adiós Mi Diente)
y, Estóy Muy Linda, Visítame

Así es que "dichos" rigorosamente proclaman la ternura del dueño o chofer
sobre muchos aspectos diferentes de un mundo circundario. Otra categoría
grande incluye animales, pájaros, fantasmas y las caricaturas:

Búfalo Rojo; o, Pato-Cito;
o, El Duende; y Papa Pitufo.

Ocasionalmente, un camionero pintará una media docena de "dichos" sobre su
vehículo; el registro es diez y seis, sobre dos camiones panameños de un dueño
aficionado. Caló se usa frecuentamente. Ortografía incorrecta y letras opuestas
son muy comunes. Algunos "dichos" simplemente no pueden ser traducidos por
el observador casual: sólo el chofer-artista sabe lo que se dice.

He intentado usar un formato consistente durante este libro. Cada capítulo está
dividido en secciones por país y por la ciudád más cercana en donde vi y recordé
el dicho. El dicho aparece primero en su forma original, casi siempre en Español,
exactamente como apareció en el vehículo, aunque sin las letras opuestas. La ortografía incorrecta original ha sido preservada. A veces son, así mismos, en-
tretenidos o introducen ambigüedad:

Estando Bien con Diós Me Vio (Fio) de los Habladores

The type of vehicle bearing the *dicho* has also been noted since that in itself can be humorous:

El Rey del Camino / King of the Road

seen on a small pickup truck!

Immediately below or alongside of each *dicho* appears an English translation. Every effort has been made to capture not only the original sense but also the known or apparent intent and flavor. Most of the time, this has been easy to accomplish, although not many drivers of moving vehicles were readily available to me for an explanation of a particularly confusing *dicho*. In some cases I have suggested more than one meaning, based upon the setting and conditions under which I observed and recorded the *dicho*. In some, I have added an enlightening comment, as with "Moby Dick": apparently, the driver of this pure white, 10,000 liter fuel truck felt that it resembled a well-known whale!

I have concluded this book with two special chapters. One is called Retazos: Odds and Ends. In it appear those *dichos* which belong in two or more chapters, or which do not really fit anywhere else. They represent a wide variety of subjects. The other, shorter chapter is called ¿Quién Sabe?: Who Knows?, and is included out of respect for the driver-artist who had taken considerable trouble to paint the particular *dicho* on his truck, sometimes ornately and with great care. With help from my books, and from many friends both here and south of the border, I have suggested a translation where one was even possible.

The amplification of this collection of *dichos* into an expanded edition is my ongoing interest as I travel in Mexico, in Brazil and in more of the Latin Americas. Since authenticity is an important criterion for this collection, along with humor and poignancy, any reader who has seen an authentic new *dicho*, or "who knows" what a Quién Sabe means, and will communicate this to the author, will be much appreciated. If possible, there should be documentation of the kind of vehicle and the place where the *dicho* was seen, along with any other information which helps in the translation and the understanding of its meaning and humor. A photograph could be of great help. All information should be addressed to:

DICHOS - Grant La Farge
P.O. Box 6132 / Santa Fe, NM 87502-6132 / USA

I would like to acknowledge and to give my heartfelt thanks to the many people who have given so generously of their time and their support in the preparation of this book:

Most especially, to Patricia Arscott La Farge, my wife, whose idea this book was and who has helped me frequently in recording *dichos*, all the while giving me unflagging encouragement;

In New Mexico: to Bernadette Rodríguez, who reviewed the manuscript, who helped to translate and to make sense of some of the Mexican *dichos*, and who

El modelo de vehículo que porta el dicho también está notado, como eso, entre si mismo, puede ser humeroso:

El Rey del Camino / *King of the Road* (a small pickup truck!)

Inmediamente abajo, o al lado de cada dicho aparece una traducción al inglés. Cada esfuerzo se ha hecho para captar no sólo el sentido original pero también la intención y el sabor conocido o evidente. La mayor parte del tiempo, esto ha sido fácil completar; aunque no pude hablar sobre la explicación de algún dicho perplejo con muchos de los choferes que caminaban en la carretera. En algunos casos he sugerido más de un sentido, bajo las condiciones alrededor donde observé y noté el dicho. En algunos, he añadido algún comentario iluminado, como el de *Moby Dick;* aparentemente, el chofer de este camión blanco de 10,000 litros de petróleo sintió que su camión parecía una ballena bién conocida!

He concluído el libro con dos capítulos especiales, uno llamado "Retazos." En este aparecen los "dichos" que pertenecen en dos o más capítulos, o que realmente no se adaptan en otra parte. Representan una variedad amplia de sujetos. El otro capítulo, más corto, se llama "Quien Sabe?" y está incluído para dar respecto al chofer-artista que habia tomado molestia considerable para pintar este dicho particular sobre su camión, a veces floridamente y con mucho cuidado. Con la ayuda de mis libros, y muchos amigos de aquí y del sur de la frontera, he sugerido una traducción donde fue posible.

La amplificación de esta colección de dichos a una edición más extendida es mi interés según viajo en Mexico, en Brasil, y en más de los países Latino-americanos. Ya que la autenticidad es un criterio importante para esta colección, a lo largo del humor y de la filosofía picante, cualquier lector que ha visto un dicho nuevo auténtico, o quien sepa el sentido de algún "Quien Sabe?," y quien quiera comunicar esto con el autor estaré muy agradecido. Donde se posible ha de ver documentación del modelo de vehículo y el lugar en donde vieron el dicho, junto con qualquier información que ayudará en el traducción y el entendemiento del sentido y del humor. Una fotografía será de mucha ayuda. Toda la información ha de ser dirigida a:

DICHOS — Grant La Farge
PO Box 6132, Santa Fe, New Mexico, 87502, USA

Quisiera reconocer y darle mis sinceras gracias a toda la gente que me dió libremente su tiempo y su apoyo en la preparación de este libro:

Principalmente a Patricia Arscott La Farge, mi esposa, que me dió la idea de escribir este libro y que frecuentemente me ayudó a notar dichos, siempre dándome inspiración incesante.

En Nuevo Mexico: a Bernadette Rodríguez que revisó el manuscrito, que ayudó en las traducciones y que trató de interpretar algunos de los dichos Mexicanos y que tradujó el prólogo y las introducciones de los capítulos al español; a Mário Garcia, mi amigo Guatemalteco, que me ayudó en traducir y comprender algunos dichos de su país; a Gédéon La Farge, mi hijo, a Ann y Paul Gerber, a Matthew

translated the Prologue and chapter introductions into Spanish; to Mário Garcia, my Guatemalan friend, who helped me to translate and to understand some of the *dichos* of his country; to Gédéon La Farge, my son, to Ann and Paul Gerber, and to Matthew Schwartzman, all of whom helped in the transcription of *dichos* during travels with me in Mexico; and to Gerry Rill of the Camera Shop in Santa Fe, who printed the black and white illustrations (which I had either copied onto Kodak Tech Pan 2415 film from my Kodachrome 64 slides, or photographed on Tri-X film);

In Mexico: to Enrique de la Lanza of Oaxaca, who helped me to translate and to appreciate the humor of many *dichos*;

In Guatemala: to the daughters of Mário García, Patricia and Blanca, who recorded some *dichos* for me; and to José Luís Aventura, who helped to make sense of the more difficult *dichos* we gathered together in the Terminal Market in Guatemala City;

In Peru: to my patient, enthusiastic taxi drivers, Rigo W. Luzón Murillo in Lima, and Carlos Lobatón Salcedo in Cusco.

In Ecuador: to Martha Egan of Albuquerque, New Mexico, who provided some Ecuadorian and Brazilian *dichos*; to Pete Cecere, who recorded *dichos* in Quito and loaned me a toy truck with a *dicho*; to Jill and John Ortman for the loan of toy buses and a toy airplane with *dichos*; and, to my knowledgeable and amiable taxi driver, Hugo Herrera.

And, in Panama: to two most communicative taxi drivers, Adriano Morelos (*Zapatero Paga Doble*) and Davis Peralta.

And now,

Fé - y ¡Adelante! / Have Faith - and Read Ahead!

Grant La Farge
Santa Fe, New Mexico, 1984

Schwartzman, todos quiénes me ayudaron en la transcripción de los dichos durante los viajes que hicimosa en México; y a Gerry Rill de la Camera Shop in Santa Fe que imprimió las ilustraciones en blanco y negro (que he copiado sobre Kodak Tech Pan 2415 de mis diapositivas originales en Kodachrome 64, o que he tomado sobre película Tri-X).

En Mexico: a Enrique de la Lanza Elton, de Oaxaca, que me ayudá traducir y estimar el humor de muchos dichos.

En Guatemala: a Patricia y Blanca, las hijas de Mario García, quiénes notaron algunos dichos; y a José Luis Aventura, que me ayudá interpretar los dichos más difíciles que juntamos en el Mercado Terminal, en la ciudad de Guatemala.

En Perú: a mis pacientes y entusiastas taxistas, Rigo W. Luzón Murillo (Lima) y Carlos Lobatón Salcedo (Cusco).

En Ecuador: a Martha Egan, de Albuquerque, Nuevo México, que transcribió algunos dichos ecuatorianos y brazileños; a Pete Cecere, que también transcribió dichos en Quito y me prestó un camión de juguete con dicho; a Jill y John Ortman por prestarme unos juguetes, dos autobuses y un avión, con dichos; y a mi amable y sabio taxista, Hugo Herrera;

Y en Panamá: a dos taxistas muy comunicativos, Adriano Morelos (Zapatero Paga Doble) y Davis Peralta. Y ahora:

Fe y Adelante!

Grant La Farge
Santa Fe, New Mexico, 1984

Fé en DIOS
H 6857
y... ¡Adelante!

RELIGIOSOS

Taxco: Todo te lo Debo A ti...Señor - Hagace Sr. Tu Voluntad.
I owe You Everything, Oh God — Thy Will Be Done. Both photos are from a small farm truck.

INTRODUCTION

Throughout Mexico and Latin America, the Christian God and the Christian saints are extremely powerful. Catholicism is the dominant religion, though others have brought their own gods and saints, too. In the Indian villages, many of the most important feasts are celebrated by combining the native rituals with those of the Christian Churches. God and the saints are a fundamental part of all life's activities. In Guatemala, where reference to God is common, few *dichos* refer to saints. In contradistinction, references to saints are frequent in the South American countries.

It is no surprise, then, that vehicular *dichos* so frequently are statements about God, or supplications to Him or to the saints. In this context, the use of the affectionate — but respectful — diminutive '--cita' with the virgins, should be noted. Mexicans appear relaxed to the point of making jokes about religion, such as *"Sigo Cristo — Alto al Pecado," "Follow Christ — Stop Sin."* The ultimate joke, reflecting real self-knowledge and faith in God, is the *dicho* which is the title of this book: *"Fé en Diós — y Adelante!," Have Faith in God — and Full Speed Ahead!*

La Paz: San Martin de Porres / Saint Martin of Porres
One of the most important saints in South America and the Philippines. MFT

INTRODUCCIÓN

En México y en América Latina el Dios cristiano y los santos cristianos son muy poderosos. El catolicismo es la religión dominante, aunque otros religiones han traído sus propios dióses y santos también. En los pueblos indígenos, muchas de las fiestas importantes son celebradas por la combinación de los rituales nativos con esos de las iglesias cristianas. Dios y sus santos son una parte fundamental de todas las actividades de la vida. En Guatemala, donde la referencia a Dios es común, pocos dichos serefieren a los santos. En contradistinto, referencias a los santos son frecuentes en los países Su-Americanos.

No es ninguna sorpresa, entonces, que los dichos vehiculares frecuentemente son declaraciones a Dios, o suplicas a El o a los santos. En este libro, el uso cariñoso — pero respectable — diminutivo, '--cita' a las virgenes, se ha de notar. Los Mexicanos aparecen ser relajados al punto de hacer chistes sobre la religión, como "Sigo Cristo — Alto al Pecado." El chiste fundamental, que refleja el conocimiento verdadero y la fé en Dios, es el dicho que es el título de este libro: "Fé en Diós — y Adelante!"

BOLIVIA

LA PAZ

Jesús La Luz / Jesus (is) the Light (MFT)

Cristo Es Amor el Unico Esperanza / Christ is Love — the Only Hope *(M Bus)*

Virgen de Copacabana / Virgin of Copacabana
(An important religious figure in Bolivia; fringe, M-Bus)

Somos Parte de Ti / We are part of You *(back window, bus)*

ECUADOR

QUITO

Sr. de la Santa Escuela – Christian—Piloto—Giovanni
God of the Holy Academy – Christian and Giovanni, 'Pilots' *(of this MFT)*

Diós Guia Mi Camino – Reina de Agua Santa
God Guides Me – Queen of Holy Waters (from Baños, Ecuadór; SFT)

Con Fé en Diós – y Adelante / With Faith in God We Go Forward *(MFT)*

Diós es Mi Piloto / God is My Pilot *(Bus)*
Corazón de Jesús / Love of Christ *(SFT)*

Jesús del Gran Poder / Jesus of (Has) Great Power *(MFT)*

Santa Anita / Little Saint Anna *(SFT)*

Virgen de las Candelárias – Niños Jenny-Jhon
Virgin of Candelaria – (My) Children, Jenny and John *(misspelled; MFT)*

Quito: Ruega Diós Que Buelva – Comercial Pérez – Trabajamos por Un Puñado de Dólares.
Pray to God You (It) Return(s) – Perez Company – We Work for Only a Handful of Dollars (SFT)

Quito *Reina de la Paz* Reina de las Lajas; Reina del Rosario; Otra Reina de la Paz
Queen of Peace, Queen of Lajas (Colombia), Queen of the Rosary; Another Queen of La Paz!
(Reina de..., honoring various virgins, is common in Ecuador; FTs and 1 DT)

GUATEMALA

ALMALONGA

Cristo Te Ama Amigo / Christ Loves You, Friend (MFT)

Cristo Vienen (Viene?) / Christ, They are Coming (Christ Comes?) (MFT front)
Cristo es Amigo Fiel / Christ is a Faithful Friend (back)

ANTIGUA GUATEMALA

Jeovah es Mi Pastór / Jehovah is My Shepherd (hand cart)

Del Agua Mansa Mc Libre Diós, Que de la Brava Me Guardaré Yo (bus)
From Calm Water, God Frees Me, So that I Will Be Careful of Angry Water

ESCUINTLA

Regalo de Diós / Gift of God (Bus; windshield fringe)

COATEPÉQUE

Diós Con Migo / God Be with Me (Bus; windshield fringe)

GUATEMALA

Diós es Mi Pastór / God is My Shepherd (Bus)
Diós Me Ayúdame / God Helps Me (MFT)
Guíame Señor / Guide Me, O Lord (Bus)

Soledad / Loneliness *(Virgin of Soledad; Bus)*
Diós y Fé / God and Faith *(Bus)*
Regalo de Diós / Gift of (from) God *(Bus)*
Cuídame Señor / Care for Me, God *(Bus)*
Jesús Te Ama / Jesus Loves You *(Bus)*
El Poder de Diós / The Power of God *(MFT)*

Diós en Mi Camino / God is (with me) on My Road *(Bus)*

Jehovah es Mi Pastór / The Lord (Jehovah) is My Shepherd *(Bus)*

Jesús Mi Bueno Pastór / Jesus, My Good Shepherd *(Bus)*

JEHOVAH ES MI PASTÓR – NADA ME FALTARÁ
Jehovah is my Shepherd – I Shall Not Want *(M-Fs, MFT)*

Que Diós Te Replique lo Que Te Desees
May God Answer (your prayers) with What You Wish *(Bus)*

*Guatemala: Diós Me Guía – Diós Bendiga Mi Camino. God Guides Me – God Bless my Highway.
Above, a very fancy cortina, or 'fringe.' These are often stitched with great care and ornateness.
In spite of the pleas for help from Above, this Bus from the Reina de las Flores line
had broken down on one of Guatemala City's busiest boulevards!*

GUATEMALA

Jesús — Maria — José / Jesus — Mary — Joseph *(MFT)*

Diós es Amor / God is Love
(Trucks and Buses in general, and one Toyota Land Cruiser! Often, this dicho is embroidered gaudily on the fringe which decorates the windshield)

Siempre la Fé en Diós / Always (have) Faith in God *(Bus)*

DIÓS ME GUÍA / God Guides Me *(MFT; on M-Fs, very elaborate paintings of volcanoes)*

Diós Me Guía – Diós Proverderá / God Guides Me - God Will Provide for Me
(On an MFT, Terminal Market)

El Divino Maestro me Accompañe -Pintor
-Mario '83
The Divine Master Accompanies Me - Painter: Mario, 1983 *(PT)*

Diós Te Cuida Bellita / God Keeps You, Little Beauty *(Bus)*

Que Diós Te Cuida - Abusadora / May God Care for You - A-BUS-er *(Bus)*

Diós Mio en Ti Confio / My God, I Have Faith In You *(Bus)*

Fé en Diós y Adelante – Pero no Chilla
Faith in God and Forward – Don't Be Offended! *(front and back respectively, Bus)*

Sigo El Rey Siendo / I Follow the King as I Am *(Horse-drawn cart)*

MAZATENANGO

Diós es Amór – Martita / God is Love – Little Martha *(Bus)*

QUETZALTENANGO

Pa Tu Sagrado Conosimiento – Diós Me Guía
For Your Sacred Knowledge – God Guides Me *(front of orange MFT)*

Guatemala: Sonrie DIÓS nos ama / Smile, God Loves Us.
A white panel truck with a young, unsmiling driver! Also seen as Sonrie Diós Te Ama / Smile, God Loves You, on the side of a "Sonrisa Line" Bus.

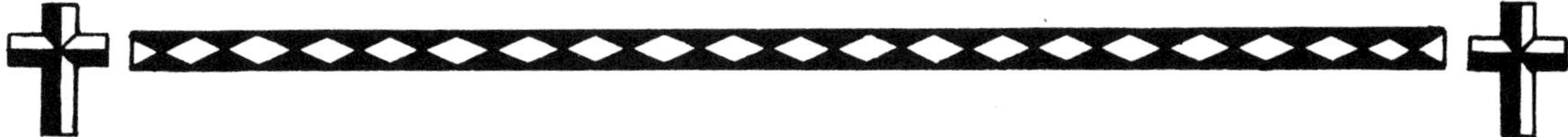

Guatemala: LLEVAME — CONTIGO / Take Me — With You.
The mudflaps of a red farm truck, parked near the Terminal Market in Guatemala City,
with the decal, En Diós Confio on the windshield. Photograph was taken at dusk, by electronic flash.

SAN JUAN SUCHITEPÉQUEZ
Jehovah Me Guía / Jehovah Guides Me *(Bus, windshield fringe)*

SANTA LUCIA COTZUMALGUAPA
Diós Bendiga Este Bus / God Bless this Bus *(Windshield fringe)*

TECPÁN
Guíame Señor / Guide Me, Lord *(Bus, windshield fringe)*

ZUNÎL
Diós es Mi Copiloto – Suq / God is My Copilot – Suq *(nickname) (Bus)*

MEXICO

ACAPULCO
Mi Miño Jesús / My Son, Jesus *(Truck; florid Gothic script!)*

ACAPULCO
Alma de Niña / Soul of a Girl *(MFT)*
Diós por Delante / Onward with God *(SFT)*
Diós Dirá / God Will Speak! *(MFT)*
Todo este Debo a Diós / I Owe God All *(SFT)*
Ayúdame Diós Mio / Help Me, My God *(MFT)*
Jesús Nazareth / Jesus (of) Nazareth *(DT)*

Bendice el Camino, Señor / Bless This Road, Oh Lord *(MFT)*

Todo Este Selo Debo a Diós / All This I Owe To God *(MFT)*
(It isn't clear if "Selo" changes the sense; perhaps "solo" - or another - word was intended:
I Owe ONLY to God)

No Falta Diós en Mi Camino / God is not Missing on My Journey *(PT)*

ACATLÁN
Sin Cristo Nada Soy / Without Christ I am Nothing *(SFT)*

Cuídanos, Señor Del Calvario / Protect Us, Lord of Calvary *(MFT)*

BERMEJILLO
Ayudala — — Señor / Help Her, Lord! *(MFT)*

BUCERIAS
Padre Nuestro / Our Father *(18-T)*
Fé en Diós y Llegaremos / Have Faith in God and We'll Get There! *(DT)*

CEBALLOS
Una Cruz en Mi Camino / A Cross in My Highway
(A play on words? Cruce is 'cross-road' usually, but...) (MFT)
In God I Trust / Tengo Fé en Diós *(LFT)*

CHILPANCINGO
Cuídame Diós del Calvário / Care for Me, God of Calvary
(Coca Cola truck; dichos are rare on soft-drink or beer trucks)
Relicario / Reliquary *(MFT)*

Lo Que Diós Quiera / That Which God Wishes (He Does)
(Could also refer directly to the vehicle, an MFT)

CIUDAD JUÁREZ
Cristiano / Christian *(18-T)*

CUAUTLA
Diós y Adelante – Yo en Volante / Faith in God; Let's Go: I'm Flying!
(also, I'm in Charge, from 'Volante,' a flywheel) (MFT)

Señor Jesús Rey Nuestro / Jesus, Our King *(DT)*

Chilpancingo: Si De Diós Hablaron Que No Dirán de Mi?
If They Spoke of God, Why Won't They Speak of Me?
Parked by the side of the road, this large, red farm truck had no driver in sight

CUERNAVACA
Diós Mio! / My God *(PTs and FTs)*
Creo en Diós / I Believe in God *(DT)*

Diós Guía Mi Camino / May God Guide My Way *(MFT)*

CUILAPAN
Cuidame Virgencita de Juquilita / Care for Me, Little Virgin of Juquila *(PT)*

FRESNILLO
Diós Vendiga Mi Camino / God Bless My Highway *(broken down MFT!)*

GOMEZ PALACIO
Divina Ilusion / Divine Illusion *(18-T)*
Jesús de Ecuadór / Jesus of Ecuador *(18-T)*
San Antonio / Saint Anthony *(18-T)*

IGUALA
Diós Me Libre / God Set Me Free *(MFT)*
Maria – José / Mary – Joseph *(MFT)*

Primero Diós y Adelante / First of All, God, then Let's Go! *(MFT)*

IXTAPAN DE LA SAL
Primero Diós – Volveré! / God Willing – I Shall Return! *(SFT)*

IZUCAR DE MATAMOROS
Diós Bendiga Mi Camino / God Bless My Way *(MFT)*

Sr. Jesús, Rey Nuestro / Señor Jesus, Our King *(MFT)*

Diós Te Doble de lo Que Me Desees..! /
May God Give You Double What You Desire for Me! *(Positive or Negative?) (PT)*

IZUCAR DE MATAMOROS
Diós de Sagrado Carazón Ilumine Mi Camino /
Light My Way, God of the Sacred Heart! *(MFT)*

Maria de los Angeles / Maria of the Angels *(18-T)*

Cuidalos, Virgencita / Care for Them, Little Virgin *(SFT)*

Sr. Ten Piedad en Mi / Señor (Christ) Have Faith in Me *(LFT)*

MOCTEZUMA
Diós Entiendele / God Understands You *(MFT)*
El Niño / The Child (Jesus Christ) *(18-T)*

OAXACA
Grácias a Diós / Thanks Be to God *(PT)*

Jesús – Jesús / Jesus – Jesus *(Truck, windshield fringe)*

Fé en Diós de los Habladores Nada
Have Faith in God, but Chatterers, None *(SFT)*

Que Me Desea Que Diós Te lo Multiplique
How I Wish that God (Would) Multiply It (or, Your Kind) *(MFT)*

Fé en Diós y Adelante – "Julissa" / Have Faith in God, Let's Go – Julissa *(MFT)*

Fé in Diós y Adelante – "Armandito"
Have Faith in God and Let Her Rip – Little Armando *(PT)*

Diós y Adelante Yo en el Volante
(Have Faith in) God and Forward I go, Flying *(PT)*

Diós Me Guía – The Lord Guides Me *(MFT)*
Mi Relicario / My Reliquary *(MFT)*
Siémpre Resa Por Mi / Always Pray for Me *(PT)*
Bendito Sea Diós / Blessed Be the Lord *(PT)*
Principe de la Paz / Prince of Peace *(Bus)*

Irapuato: En Diós Comfio Por Eso Vuelvo. / I have Faith in God – This Time Around! (MFT)

Ayudame Diós Mio / Help Me, My God *(DT)*
San Juan Niño / Saint John, the Child *(SFT)*
Rey de Reyes / King of Kings *(DT)*

Diós Mio – – Cuidala! / Oh My Lord – – Take Care of Her! *(PT)*

Recuerdo Juquila / I Remember the Virgin of Juquila *(MFT)*

Estando Bién con Diós Me Vio de Los Habladores / Being 'in good' with God,
I Can Recognize (Am Free of, 'Fío') the Gossipers *(MFT)*

Sagrado Corazón de Jesús En Ti Confio
Oh Sacred Heart of Jesus, My Confidence is in You! *(PT)*

Alludame – Diós Mio – "Lupita" – Cuidame Virgencita de Juquila
Help Me, My God! – Little Guadalupe – Care for Me, Little Virgin of Juquila
(MFT)

Diós Vendiga el Trabajo del Valle / God Bless the Work of the Valley
(of Oaxaca) *(MFT)*

En Diós Mi Fé en Ti Mi Esperanza / In God My Faith, in Thee, My Hope *(MFT)*

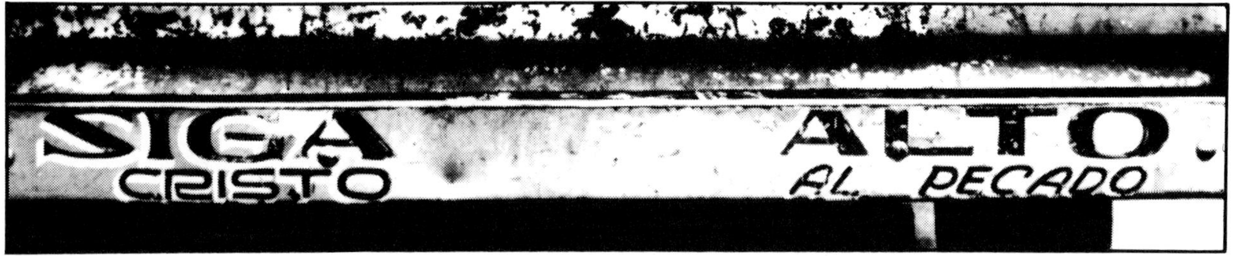

Oaxaca: SIGO Cristo – ALTO al Pecado / Follow Christ – Stop Sin.
*This hard-used pickup truck, without mudflaps, displayed a variation on a common,
Mexican mudflap instruction, which appears in the photograph on page 117:*

Liberame Domine et Inimicus – De la Mañana
Free Me, Oh Lord, and Mine Enemy – From Tomorrow!
(The first part on the hood, the rest on the bumper) *(MFT)*

Preferencia Virgen de Juquilita / Pre-eminence to the Virgin of Juquila
(or, She's My Choice) *(MFT)*

Diós Eterno Accompaños Siempre / Eternal God, Accompany Us Always *(MFT)*

Crus de Olvido / Cross of Oblivion (with slanted "†") *(Bus)*

Diós Mio Te Confio / My Lord, I have Faith in Thee *(MFT)*

Primero Diós – Bolveré si El Me Cuida
God First – I Shall Return if He Cares For Me *(SFT)*

OAXACA
Una Plegaria a Diós por un Feliz Regresso
A Supplication to God for a Happy Return *(PT)*

Hagace Señor Tu Voluntad – "Juancito" / Let Thy Will Be Done – Little Juan *(PT)*

Diós Te Salve – Margarita / God Save You – Margarita
(dicho on front bumper; name on the hood) *(SFT)*

Ayudame Diós Mio – Alma Zapoteca / Help Me, My Lord – Zapotecan Soul *(MFT)*

Señor de la Humilidad / Man of Humility *(LFT)*

Diós Te Bendiga – StMa Trinidad / God Bless You – St. Mary of Trinidad *(SFT)*

Primero Diós en Mi Camino / First of All, God (is) on My Highway *(DT)*

Señor Ten Piedad de Nosotros – Solo Me Derrite Venme a Traer por Cachitas
God, Have Pity on Us – Only You are Loving to Me so that I May Come
to You for Small Favors (Cachitas is probably from Gachas) *(MFT)*

Si de Diós Hablarón Que no Hablarán de Mi
If They Spoke of God, Why Will They Not Speak of Me? *(SFT)*

Oh Gran Diós – Negro / Oh Great God – Black (Or, 'Oh Great Black God.')
(Back, front bumpers. Both parts of *dichos* sometimes must be read as one!) *(MFT)*

Ilumina Mi Camino Virgencita de Juquila – Barotero 29 / Illumine my Way,
Little Virgin of Juquila – Cheap Sales No. 29 *(truck with cheap clothes)*

*Oaxaca: DIÓS ME GUÍA – MURMUREN / Guide Guides Me – They are Gossiping.
Fancy Mudflaps on a PT*

Como el Castigo de Diós Tarde Pero Llego – Virgencita de Mi Soledad / Like the Punishment of God, I'm Late, but Here I am! – Little Virgin of my Solitude
(The latter is a double entendre: La Virgen de la Soledad is the most important religious figure in Oaxaca) (SFT)

!!Diós Es Amor¡¡ – El Salvador / God Is Love! – The Savior
(The exclamation points were upside down: incorrect usage) (SFT)

Conquistador del Cielo / Conqueror of Heaven (the Sky) (18-T)

PÁTZCUARO
† Cristo Roto † / Christ Destroyed (MFT)

PUEBLA
Quién Como Diós / There's No One Like God (MFT)

Cuidame Virgensita / Care for Me, Little Virgin (misspelled) (SFT)

San Juan Bautista / Saint John the Baptist (MFT)

PUERTO VALLARTA
Fé en Diós y Adelante – "Lilia" / Have Faith in God and Let's Go! – Lilia (DT)
Maria de Luz / Holy Mary of the Light (Bus)
Que Diós Te Perdone / May God Forgive You (Bus)

Diós en Mi Camino / God is (With Me) On My Way (MFT)

Suerte y Benedición de Diós / Good Fortune and Blessing from God (MFT)

SAMALAJARA
Santa Teresita / Little Saint Theresa (MFT)

SAN CRISTOBAL DE LAS CASAS
Que Diós Te Bendiga / May God Bless You (MFT)
Reliquario Dos / Reliquary Number 2 (MFT)

Diós Me Guíame en Mi Camino / God Guides Me On My Way (MFT)

Diós Arriba Yo Abajo / God (is) Above, I (am) Below (MFT)

SAN GABRIÉL CHILÁC
San Juán de Los Lagos / Saint John of the Lakes (MFT)

Sonrie Cristo Te Ama – San Gabriel / Smile, God Loves You – Saint Gabriel
(LFT)

SAN LUIS POTOSÍ
Santa – Rita / Saint Margaret (MFT)

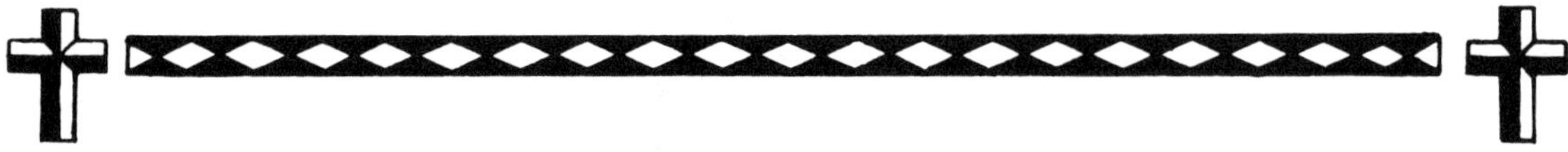

San Cristobal de las Casas: Fé en Diós y Adelante / Faith in God and Full Speed Ahead
The dog did not think that this farm truck
was going anywhere "Full Speed Ahead" on a cloudy, drizzly day in San Cristobal!

SANTA MARIA DEL RIO
Divina Ilución / Divine Illusion (18-T)

SAN MIGUÉL DE ALLENDE
God's Drivin' / Diós Maneja (Van from Guanajuato)

TAMAZULAPAM
Ruega Por Me / Pray for Me (MFT)

TAXCO
Primér Diós! / God Above All (MFT)
La Purisima / The Purest One (MFT)
Padre Diós / God The Father (MFT)
Mis Carmelitas / My Flowers (ladies) (SFT)

Fé en Diós – y ¡Adelante! / Have Faith in God – Full Speed Ahead! (MFT)

Cuídame, Virgencita de Guadalupe / Take Care of Me, Virgin of Guadalupe
(MFT)

Cuídalo, Santa Prisca / Protect it (him), Saint Prisca (The MFT)

Cuídanos, Santa Prisca / Take Care of Us, Saint Prisca (MFT)

Solo Diós Sabe Mi Destino / Only God Knows My Destiny (MFT)

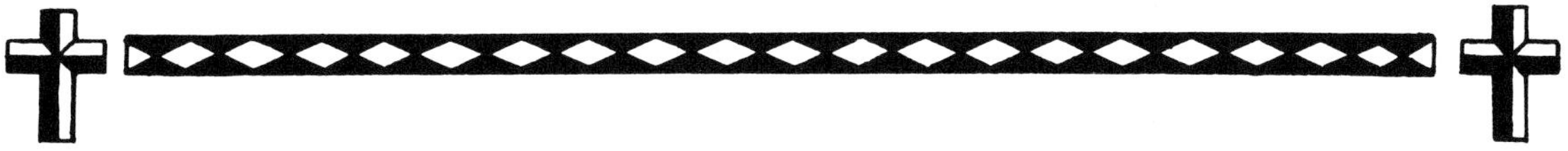

Guíanos, Sr. de Petál / Guide us, Señor (God) of Petál (LFT)

MA DE LA LUZ / Maria of the Light (cab top) (MFT)

El Hijo de los Milagros / The Son of Miracles (SFT)

Diós y Guardí / (I Believe in) God and I'm Saved! (VW 'Bug')

En Ti Fio Diós Mio / I Have Faith in You, God (SFT)

TEHUACÁN
Cordero de Diós / Lamb of God (MFT)

TIERRA COLORADA
Apostól Trece / The Thirteenth Apostle (MFT)

Bendice Mi Camino Señor / Bless My Highway, Lord (MFT)

TOLUCA
Te Vas Bendiga Mia – Dios Te Salve
You Are My Blessed One – God Save You (An example of front and back connection)
(SFT)

TUXPÁN
San Simón / Saint Simon (LFT)

Taxco: * Primero Diós * – # Pepe y Mário # / God Above All – Pepe and Mario
This Taxco dump truck (receiving debris from adjacent construction) took no chances,
and covered its religious needs both verbally and pictorially

TUXTLA GUTIERREZ
Diós Me Proveerá / God will Provide For Me *(PT)*

Regalo De Cielo / Gift from Heaven *(MFT)*
Diós Bendiga / God Blesses (You) *(MFT)*

Regalo De Reyes / Cift of the Magi *(18-T)*

YERMO
El Negro José & El Negro José II / Black Joe & Black Joe No. 2) *(Two FTs)*

ZACATECAS
Diós Me Guía / God Guides Me *(PT)*
Cristo Rey / Christ (the) King *(18-T)*
Padre Nuestro / Our Father *(Bus)*
Que Diós Te Ayude / May God Help You *(LFT)*

PANAMA

PANAMÁ
Bendígame Todo lo que Estoy Caminando / Bless Me Everywhere I Travel
(painting of Christ on back door) *(Bus)*

El MANDAMAS – Shalom / The Big Shot – Shalom (The former could be "HE
Sends Us More!; the latter was accompanied by a painting of a Star of David, back door) *(Bus)*

Solo le Pido Perdona á Diós – Diseñado por Conquistar
I Only Ask that God Pardon You (front) – Designed for Conquest! (back) *(Bus)*

San Miguel Arcangel II / Saint Michael, Archangel
(with painting of Charles Bronson, back door) *(Bus)*

Diós Es Amor – Conversa! / God Is Love – Live! (back, front) *(Bus)*

Fé en Todo – Grácias á Diós / Faith in Everything – Thanks (Be) to God
(front, back) *(Bus)*

Diós Mio Líbrame de Todo Mal / God Frees Me of Everything Bad *(Bus)*

La Milagrosa / The Miraculous one
(with painting of Virgin) (back door) *(Bus)*

Panama: Salmo 23 Jehová es mi pastor, con el nada me faltará – Así es La Vida
Psalm 23: The Lord Is My Shepherd, with Him I Shall Not Want – That's Life! (back bumper) (Bus)

Panama: Con Fé y …Confianza – Diós Es Amor…Buscalo
With Faith and …Confidence – God is Love …Look for Him (back, front) (MFT)

Protegenos – Gran Señor / Protect Us – Great God (back, side) *(Bus)*

Fé en el Futuro – Castigando / Faith in the Future – Chastising (or 'correcting,')
(back, front) *(Bus)*

Sonrie Jesús Te Ama – Virgen del Carmen / Smile, Jesus Loves You
– Virgin of Carmen (the latter is important in Panama) (back, side) *(Bus)*

Libranos de Mal / Deliver Us from Evil (painting of Christ on back door) *(Bus)*

San Antonio Milagroso / Saint Anthony, Miracle Worker *(Taxi)*

Diós con Nosotros / God Be with Us *(SFT)*

PERU

CUSCO
Diós es Amor y Esperanza / God Is Love and Hope *(Bus)*

Guíame Sr. de Luren – Virgen de Fatima
Guide Me Jesus of Luren – Virgin of Fatima (A lot of power being invoked!) *(Bus)*

Sr. de Ccoylliti Guíame / Jesus of Ccoylliti, Guide Me *(MFT)*

Diós es Amor – Urqueño / God Is Love – Man from Urcos
(Trucks and buses often have acknowledgmeent of origen) *(MFT)*

Diós Tarda pero Nunca Olvida – Fray Martin
God Takes His Time, but Never Forgets – Brother Martin *(MFT)*

Virgen de las Dolores / Virgin of the Sorrows *(MFT)*

LIMA
Sin Cristo No Soy Nadie / Without Christ, I am Nobody *(Bus)*

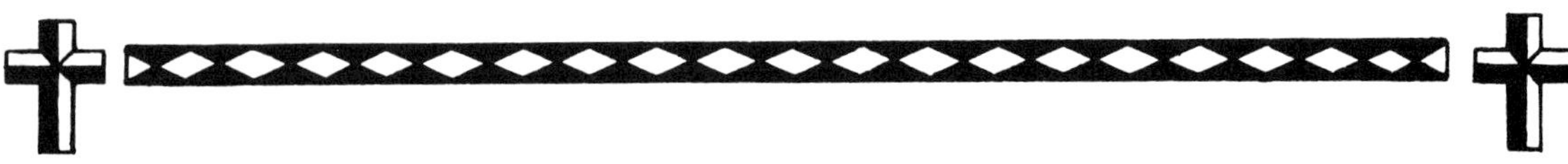

*Lima: *Diós*Es*Mi*Guia* / God Is My Guide*
This bus and its jovial driver (on the right) also provided the dicho for the back cover of this book:
Hasta La Victoria Final / Until the Final Victory!

LIMA
Devoto de San Miguel / Devoted to Saint Michael (old SFT)

Mi Fé Niño Jesús / My Faith (Is in) Baby Jesus (MFT)

Immaculada Concepción / Immaculate Conception (SFT)

Virgen de: Candelaria; Chapi No. 1; Las Dolores; Cacharcas; Sr. de: Chalpan;
Cautivo; Chocan; Los Milagros; Huanca; La Asunción
(These virgins and Christs, and many more, are as commonly observed as they are important)

Cristo Morado / The Purple Christ (Feast of October 18th to 28th) (Bus)

Primer Mandamiento – Sr. Tu Eres Mi Guia
First Commandment – Lord You Are My Guide (Bus)

Guíame Sr. Padre Eterno / Guide Me, Oh Eternal Father (MFT)

San Antonio de Padua / Saint Anthony of Padua (Bus)

Cristo Divino / Divine Christ (MFT)

Lima: Guíame Señor Cautivo / Guide Me, Christ, Captive Among the Infidels (MFT)

Dichos con
AMOR y AMORES

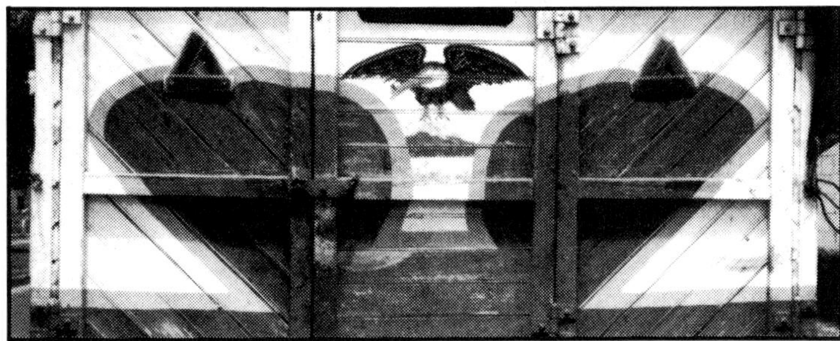

Quito: Demite Olvidaras pero de lo Que Hisimos Jamas – Si Diós Quiere Volveré – Fabiancito.
You Will Forget Me but Never what We Did Together – If God Wishes, I Shall Return – Little Fabian
(MFT)

INTRODUCTION

Love is a universal quality which pervades all dichos, even the absolutely religious: they have holy love. Love and God seem to be the forces which move the Latin soul beyond all else, sometimes in combination, as in:

Dios Conmigo y Yo Contigo / God is with Me, and I'm with You!

In all its forms – requited, unrequited, hopeless, angry, humorous, passionate – Love will be found in all the Chapters in this book: every variation on the theme of Love and Lovers is represented. There is even a play on sounds:

TBC & TDG / I Kissed You and Left You
Another version of this is cited by Jiménez in *Picardia Mexicana:*
T BC & T DG 1 BB / I Kissed You and Left You One Baby!

Jimenez also refers to Guatemala, "where the customs of the drivers are so distinct from those of ours here [in Mexico], that they inscribe on their trucks tender epigrams like (this) with flavor and saccharin: *LA LUZ DE TUS OJOS ME GUÍA.*" (Jiménez, page 14).

Guatemala: *Nóvia del Sheik / The Sheik's Girlfriend*
Seen in the Terminal Market, where people and produce arrive in the city by bus from outlying towns.

INTRODUCCIÓN

El amor es la calidad universal que penetra todos los dichos, hasta los más religiosos: estos tienen amor sagrado. El amor y Dios aperecen ser as fuerzas que mueven ante todo el alma latina, a veces en combinación como:

Diós Conmigo y Yo contigo!

En todas sus formas – satisfecho, insatisfecho, desesperado, enfadado, humorístíca, apasionado – el amor se encontrará en todos los capítulos de este libro: cad variación sobre el tema del amor y amores está representado. Hasta hay un juego sobre sonidos:

TBC Y TDG / Te Besé y Te Dejé.
Otra versión de este está citado por Jiméinez en *Picardia Mexicana*
T BC & T DG 1 BB / Te Besé y Te Dejé en Bebé!

Jiménez también refiere a Guatemala, "donde las costumbres de los choferes son tan distintas de las que tienen los conductores de aquí [en México], que escriben en sus camiones tiernos epígrafes como éstos con sabor a sacarina: *LA LUZ DE TUS OJOS ME GUÍA.*" (pagina 14).

BRAZIL

CARAUARÚ
Beijo da Mulher Casada Tem Sabor de Chumbo
The Kiss of a Married Woman Tastes of Lead *(MFT)*

ECUADOR

OTAVALO
Yo y Tu / You and I *(SFT)*
LOVE – Amor *(On the hood of a MFT)*

Mi Gitano – Es Un Ford / My Gypsy – It's a Ford!
(This latter is very common in Ecuador) (MFT)

Piensame No Me Olvides / Think of Me, Don't Forget Me *(PT)*

Medico de las Solteras – Reina de Agua / Doctor to the Lonely Ladies
(Includes free examination! — another Virgin) (MFT)

Llego Mi Amor / I Arrive, My Love (or) My Love Arrived *(SFT)*

Jurame Que No Me Engañas / Swear to Me that You Deceive Me Not *(MFT)*

QUITO
Tu Cariñito / Your Beloved *(LFT)*
Estoy Sufriendo / I'm Suffering *(MFT)*
Siempre Solo / Always Alone *(Bus)*
Amor Libre / Free Love! *(Bus)*

Yo Soy Aquel Que Llora Durante tu Ausencia? – Don Pablito
I'm One of Those who Cries When You Are Gone? – Little Paul
(This was written in the mud on the back of a large petroleum truck)

Corazón No Te Desesperes / Do Not Despair, My Love *(MFT)*

Amor Subirse en Este Camion…Sola!
Climb into this Truck, Love…Alone! *(LFT)*

Pensate Que No Va Volver / You (Only) Think You Aren't Returning *(SFT)*

Negrita Linda Me Voy Pero Volveré
My Lovely Dark One, I Go but I'll Return *(Bus)*

Así te Prometí Norma Mia / That's What I Promised You, Norma Mine *(MFT)*

Sufriras Mientras Yo Viva [Corazón] / You Will Suffer While I Live, My Love
(Only a picture of a heart for [corazón]) (LFT)

QUITO

La Mujer Maravillosa – Maria Ketyta / The Marvellous Woman – Maria Ketyta
(MFT)

Sigame Que Te Espero / Follow Me: I'm Waiting *(MFT)*

Fui Tuyo Fuiste Mio / I Was Yours; You Were Mine *(SFT)*

Chulita – La Envidia Te Mata / Cutie – Jealousy Will Kill You *(MFT)*

Lloraras Cuando Yo Muera / You Will Cry When I Die *(LFT)*

Cuando Me Miras con Dolor Suspiras – El Medico de Las Solteras
When You Look At Me You Will Sigh with Pain – Doctor to the Lonely Ladies
(MFT)

Antigua Guatemala: Aquí Estóy Mi Amor Carolina
Carolina / Here I Am Carolina, My Love – Carolina
Good Friday, and dawn found Carolina and her lover amorously juxtaposed at the
Merced Cathedral Market. Pushcarts for delivering merchandise of all kinds.

GUATEMALA

ANTÍGUA GUATEMALA
Suavecito / Little Smooth One *(MFT)*
Pecadora / Sinner (Female) *(Bus)*

Si No Me Quieres Me Mato / If You Don't Love Me, I'll Kill Myself *(MFT)*

Amores de Lejos es de Pendejos
Someone Who Has Loves in Far off Places (and presumably is married) is a Skunk
or Long Distance Love Affairs are for Fools (PT)

Ojos Que No Ven Corazón Que No Siente
(One With) Eyes which See Without Love Feels Nothing *(MFT)*

Amor con Amor se Paga / Love That is Truly Love, Pays *(MFT)*

Guatemala: Muchacho Solitário / Lonely Bachelor
This large farm truck was parked by the side of one of the very busiest of the city's thoroughfares.

GUATEMALA
Orgullosa y Bonita / Proud and Beautiful *(Bus)*
El Mil Amores / The Thousand Lovers *(PT)*

Se Me Amas, No Me Reculas / If You Love Me, Don't Recoil From Me *(MFT)*

Diós Conmigo Y Yo Contigo / God is with Me, and I'm with You! *(Bus)*

EN CADA VIAJE – UN AMOR / On Every Trip – A (new) Love *(MFs) (MFT)*

Si Tu Me Odias, Diós No Me Olvida
If You Hate Me, God Will Not Forget Me *(Bus)*

Si Me Odias, Por Que Sufres as Verme?
If You Hate Me, Why Suffer to See Me? *(MFT)*

Sufres al Verme / You('ll) Suffer When You See Me *(Bus)*

Sufres Mi Auséncia / You Suffer (in) My Absence *(Bus)*

GUATEMALA

Nunca Te Olvides de Mi / You (Must) Never Forget Me *(MFT & Bus)*

Chavo Sin Compromiso / Bachelor Without Commitments *(Flatbed lumber truck)*

La Llevo Pero Sola / I'll Give Her a Lift, but Alone! *(on Vehicles!)*

Cuídame Si Puedes / Care for Me – If You Can *(Bus)*

Vino Mujér y Tabaco Dejan al Ombre Bién Flaco
Wine, Women and Tobacco Leave a Man Very Weak *(Frail, dejected, lazy) (Bus)*

Olvídame Si Puedes – Pitufina / Forget Me If you Can – Lady Smurf *(Bus)*

Alcansame Si Puedes / Catch Me if You Can *(Bus)*

Que Culpa Tengo –– Lo Que Me Quierran
How Guilty I Am –– They Love Me For it *(M-Bus)*

Llegarán Las Preferidas / The Preferred Ones (Ladies?) Have Arrived
(On a Bus of the Preferida Bus Line)

Preciosa – y ¿Que? / Precious – and What Else? *(Bus of the Preciosa Bus Line)*

MIRATE Y – CRITICAME / First Look at Me – Then Criticize *(Mudflaps) (SFT)*

MAZATENANGO

Sufro Tu Auséncia / I Suffer (in) Your Absence *(MFT)*

QUETZALTENANGO

Mi Amorcita / My Love *(Very tender!) (MFT)*

SALCAJÁ

Chatia Preferida / Preferred Cutie *(Bus)*

MEXICO

ACATLÁN

Mi Pequeña Consentida / My Little Pampered One *(VW 'Bug')*
El Aventurero / The Adventurer *(MFT)*

ACAPULCO

Recuérdame / Remember Me! *(Bus)*
Amor Ardiente / Ardent Love *(Bus)*
Mi Prieto / My Swarthy One *(MFT)*

AGUAS CALIENTES

Ella á Su Lado y Yo Azúl Lado
She's (Staying) On Her Side and (so) I'm on the Blue Side (I've Got the Blues)
(A play on the words á Su Lado and Azúl Lado) (MFT)

AXIXINTLA
Recuerdame Mia Bea / Remember Me, My Beautiful! (For Bella) *(Bus)*

CHILPANCINGO
Me Sobre Todavia Corazón / I Have Heart to Spare *(MFT)*
Te Quiero Tanto / I Love You So *(MFT)*

Amor Te De Una Noche / My Love, I'll Give You One Night *(MFT)*

CIUDAD JUÁREZ
Mi Destino Fué Quererte y Mi Desgrácia Mantenerte
My Destiny Was to Love You and My Misfortune, to Keep You *(PT)*

Oaxaca: Que tal te va sin Mi / How are you doing without Me?
Does the "Me" refer to the Christ whose picture, with the Sacred Heart, is underneath?
The driver of this Jeep Wagoneer has a large, happy family!

Me Ves y Sufres / You See Me and You Suffer *(MFT)*

Sufre Con Migo Pero de Hambre no Te Mueres
You (May) Suffer with Me but You Do Not Die of Hunger *(SFT)*

Vieja Pero Señorita N° 3 / Old, but Still a Miss No. 3 *(PT)*

CUAUTLA
Contigo –– O Sin Ti / With You –– or Without You *(SFT)*

ETLA
Me Voy Pero Vuelvo / I'm Leaving, but I'm Coming Back
(Scratched into the back body paint) *(MFT)*

GOMEZ PALACIO
Nomas Con Tigo – San Francisco de Assis
(I'm Going) No More with You – Saint Francis of Assisi
(No Mas, run together) *(LFT)*

GOMEZ PALACIO
Un Dia Con Otro / One Day with Another... *(LFT)*

TUXPÁN
San Simón / Saint Simon *(LFT)*

HUAJUAPAN DE LEÓN
DON JUAN / Don Juan (Enormous letters, large bumper) *(18-T)*

IGUALA
Solín / Very, Very Alone *(18-T)*
Mi Prieto / My Dark-Skinned One *(Black 18-T)*

IZUCAR DE MATAMOROS
Limisnero Mi Amor / (I'm) A Beggar, My Love
(Limosnero probably was intended) *(MFT)*

Amor Sinsero No Hay Como Maisero
More Sincere Love than a Corn Planter's There Isn't *(LFT)*

Mi Destino Fué Quererte Mi Desgrácia es Perderte –
Y Todo por No Estudiar – Coqueta / My Destiny Was to Love You;
My Misfortune Was to Lose You – And All (That) for Not Studying – Flirt
(Another front-back bumper combination with a complete message, plus accusation!
The driver said he should have known better, but lost his lady anyway!) *(SFT)*

Mi Viejito Concentido / My Li'l Ol' Spoiled One *(SFT)*

IRAPUATO
Dulce Maria / Sweet Mary *(PT)*

Mi Preferida / My Preference (for My *PT!*)

*Oaxaca: Amorcito — Corazón / Little Lover — Heart.
A heart pierced by Amor's arrow. (FT)*

Oaxaca: Ladrona De Besos — Servicio De Alquiler / Stealer of Kisses (female) — For Hire
The Ladrona was a pickup truck parked near the old Oaxaca (Benito Juárez) Market;
this type of truck is used frequently by farmers, and others, to haul light cargo in the markets.
Hence, the humorous relationship between Servicio de Alquiler and the bumper dicho!

IXTAPAN DE LA SAL
Amor Impossible – Impossible Love(r?) (SFT)
Goodbye My Love / Adiós Mi Amor (SFT)

JILÓTEPEC
Amor Y Paz / Love and Peace (DT)

MÉTEPEC
Celosa / Jealous (DT)

Oaxaca: Ladrón de Besos / Stealer of Kisses (male)
The Ladrón, a large farm truck with produce, was parked near the Central Market.

MITLA
No Te Illusiones Corazón Me Voy De Paso
Don't Kid Yourself, My Love, I'm just Passing Through *(18-T)*

MORELIA
Te Vas Mio / You're Mine! *(Bus)*

Linda Chiquita – Amigo / Pretty Little Cutie – Friend *(SFT)*

MOROLEÓN
Amor Eterno / Eternal Love *(VW Combi Wagon)*

OAXACA
Te Invito a Mi Mundo / I Invite You To My World *(MFT)*

Asi Como Me Ves Te Verás / As You See Me, So Shall You Ever *(MFT)*

Yo Te Recuerdo / I Remember You *(MFT)*
Solitario / Bachelor *(Bus)*
Liberated Woman *(very neatly; rear window) (PT)*
Así Te Quiero / I Like You as You Are *(MFT)*
Mi Querido Viejo / My Beloved Old One *(MFT)*
Te Extraño Mucho / I Miss You Terribly *(LFT)*
Vaquero de Noche / (Mid)Night Cowboy *(18-T)*
Quiéreme Siempre / Love Me always *(MFT)*
Para Que Volviste? / Why Did You Return? *(Bus)*
Chiquilita / Little Cutie *(Bus)*
Amor de Estudiante / A Student's Love *(Bus)*
Porque Me Temes / Why Do You Fear Me? *(Bus)*
Una Aventura Mas / One Adventure More *(MFT)*

Oaxaca: Si No Me Quieres Para Que Me Odias / If You Don't Love Me, Why Do You Hate Me So?
Is this battered pickup speaking for itself as well as its driver?
A great deal of care obviously went into painting not only the dicho but also the letters CHEVROLET.

Sigo Solterón / I'm Still Single! *(MFT)*
Te Regalo Mi Auséncia / I Give (gave) You My Absence *(Bus)*

El Mal Querido / (I am, or It is) the Unloved One *(Bus)*

ODÍAME – – OLVÍDAME / Hate Me – – Forget Me (Mudflaps) *(MFT)*

Chinón / Curly (assumes Chino as the basic word, meaning curly-haired, or ugly) *(MFT)*

Corazón "De" Roca / Heart of Rock (the "DE" was written as one letter) *(DT carrying rocks)*

Esperando Tu Regresso / I'm Awaiting Your Return *(MFT)*

Te Acordarás de Mi / You Shall Remember Me *(MFT)*

Por Tu Envidia Estás Sufriendo / For Your Jealousy You are Suffering *(MFT)*

Como Quieras Como Quiero / As You Would Like it, I like it *(SFT)*

Hay Envidias y También Ardores – "Carmelita"
There are Envies and Ardors! – Carmelita *(MFT)*

Amor de los Dos / Love of the Two (What or Who?) *(MFT)*

Te Tuve y Te Perdí / I Had You and I Lost You *(Bus)*

Divino Tormento – El Chiquita – Juquita / Divine Torment – Lil' One – Juquita
(MFT)

Quiereme Tal Como Soy / Love Me Just as I Am *(Bus)*

PUEBLA
Podras Dejarme…Pero Olvidarme Nunca! – Mariola
You Could Leave Me…but Forget Me? Never! – Mariola *(SFT)*

QUARENTA Y CINCO
Love / Amor (Scratched into the front bumper paint) *(LFT)*

SAN CRISTOBAL DE LAS CASAS
Si Eres Selosa No Te Enamores de El
If You're Jealous, Don't Become Enamored with Him! *(Bus)*

SAN JUÁN DE LA PAZ
En Diós Mi Fé En Ti Mi Amor / In God, My Faith, in You, My Love *(MFT)*

SAN LUIS POTOSÍ
Mi Fé en Ti / My Faith is in You *(MFT)*

SAN MIGUEL DE ALLENDE
Por Tu Recuerdo / For Your Remembering (Me) *(MFT)*

Oaxaca: Rojo de Amor Pero No de…Verguenza / Red from Loving but not from…Shame! (PT)

TAXCO
Todo Por Ti / Everything for You (Bus)
Taxco de Mis Amores / Taxco of My Love(r)s (Bus)
Todo Por Ti / Everything for You (Bus)
El Solitário / The Loner (MFT)
Besame y Olvidame / Kiss Me and Forget Me (SFT)

Amor––Caminante – Necio – Lizzet / Travelling Love(r) – Foolish – Fighter
(Assumes Lizzet is from Liza) (LFT)

Tu Bas Angel Mio / You are My Travelling Angel (Bus)

Que Tal Te Va Sin Mi / How is it Going For You Without Me (Bus)

Recuérdame Buén Ami / Remember Me, My Good Friend (Bus)

TBC & TDG (Te Besé y Te Dejé) / I Kissed You and Left You (Truck, Bus)

TECAMACHULCO
La Pobrecita / The Poor Thing! (SFT)
Pequeño Amante / Little Lover (SFT)

TEOTITLÁN
Podras Odiarme…Pero Olvidarme Jamas
You Could Hate Me, but Forget Me? Never! (PT)

Amor Perdido / Lost Love (18-T & MFT)

TEHUACÁN
Angel Negro / Black Angel (Dark brown LFT)
Tan Chulo Mi Viejo / My Old One is So Cute (Bus)

*Oaxaca: *Estelita – Honorito* / Little Stella – Honorito*
The paths of love are not always smooth. The hood of this pickup truck testified that
Honorito and Estelita were no longer on terms of affection!

Me Critican por Ardor – El Aventurero
They Criticize My Ardor – Adventurer *(MFT)*

TOLUCA
Sublime Trobador / Sublime Troubador *(DT)*

Love –– Away *(Old PT)*

Oaxaca: Te Deseo con Todo Mi Amor / I Desire You with All My Love
This dicho was etched in the glass of both doors (see also page 126) (MFT)

TUXTLA GUTIERREZ
Sufres Mi Auséncia / You Suffer (in) My Absence (MFT)

YANHUITLÁN
Llevame en Tu Pensamiento / Carry Me in Your Thoughts (PT)

ZACATECAS
Muchacho Veloz / Speedy Kid (MFT)

ZITACUÁRO
Mi Pobreza / My Poverty (SFT)

PANAMA

(Note: All AMOR Y AMORES dichos of Panamá are from Buses!)

PANAMÁ
Pensando en Ti / Thinking of You
Siempre Recordaré / I'll Always Remember
La Fuerza del Cariño / The Force of Love
Tentaciones / Temptations
Sufre en Silencio / Suffer in Silence!
Sufre Ahora – Hay de Todo / Suffer Now – There is Some of Everything
Entre Amigos – Between Friends
Llorarás y Llorarás / You'll Cry and Cry
No Lloras Mas / You'll Cry No More
Donde Estas [Corazón] / Where are you Love
Tu Lo Sabes / You Know It!
Se Bendigo Contigo Mismo / I'm Only Blessed with You

Sube––Pero Sola! / Come In––Alone!
Maldito Amor / Curséd Love, or Wicked Lover
Para Que Me Admiren / Why do They Love Me?
Soy de Todos / I'm a Little of Everything
Tu Martiro / Your Martyr (How I Suffer!)

Panamá: Sé Qué Me Odias Pero Jamás Me Olvidarás – El Chepano.
I Know Why You Hate Me but You Will Never Forget Me – Your Hunchback. (back & side, Bus)

Siempre en Mi Mente / Always on My Mind
Y Por Amores No Sufro / And, For Loves I Do Not Suffer!

No Te Alteres – Pacific Queen / Don't Change – Pacific Queen Bus Line

Quisiera – Mas Bien y Vivas / I would like – More Good and Live Ones!
(front & back)

Quisieras – Haz Bien y Viviras / I'd Like (It) – Do Good and You Will Live!
(front & back)

Solicito Amigo Amar – La Ultima Pelea
I Am Seeking a Friend to Love – The Ultimate Struggle *(front & back)*

Dime Cuando Nena / Tell Me When (you are) a Girl (and Ready!)

Te Pongo á Reir Te Pongo á Llorar / I Make You Laugh and Cry

Por Mi Llorarás – El Verdugo / For Me You'll Cry – The Hangman *(back & side)*

De Nada Val Ser Buena – Santos Fe
It's Worth Nothing to be Good (, honey) – Holy Saints! *(back & side)*

Con Todos Mis Sentimientos – Recientamente
With All My Sorrow – Lately *(front & back)*

Son Tus Celos – Un Abuso / I'm All Your Jealousy – An Imposition *(front & back)*

Esta Noche – ¡Opino Que No Te Debe Llorar!
Tonight – In My Opinion, You Won't Need to Cry
*(front & back) (This is a good example of the frequent relationship between
the dicho on the front of the bus and the one on the back)*

Amo de Belleza – [Corazón] Guerrero / I Love Beauty – I Love Guerrero
(back & front)

Tu de Repente Tu / You, Suddenly You *(with painting of Barbra Streisand on back door)*

Amor Falso No Quiere – Lo Tuyo Vanidad – Miss Violeta
You Don't Want Untrue Love – That Is Your Vain Hope! – Señorita Violet
(back, front & side) (With a painting of the movie hero Conan on the back door)

Panamá: E–No Me Compares–R – Así lo Dicen / Do Not Compare Me – So They Say
(implies incomparable) Paintings of caboose above, lady with devils below. (back, fancy Bus)

PANAMÁ
[Corazón] de Oro – Dices Que No Te Quiero
Heart (painted) of Gold – (How can) You Say I Don't Love You!? *(front & back)*

PERU

CUSCO
Corazon Contento / (My) Heart's Content *(MFT)*
El Amigo / The Friend *(MFT)*

Mi Chiquitín Sicuani / My Little Beauty from Sicuani *(MFT)*

LIMA
La Recorrida / The Journey *(SFT)*
Hola Soledad / Hello, Lonely *(18-T)*
Mi Luz Aurora / My Aurora *(MFT)*
Querer Es Poder / To Love is Power *(MFT)*
Corazón Sin Puerto / Heart with no Bar *(Bus)*
Chinita––Tu y Yo / Cutie––You and I *(MFT)*

Tu Eres Mi Esperanza *[corazón]* / You are My Hope (Esperanza), Love
(with painting of heart with arrow) *(MFT)*

Solo el Amor Es Mejor Que Leche Vigor
Only Love Is Better than Vigor Milk *(hand done on an SFT)*
(This is a case of an advertisement for powdered milk being used as a dicho)

Solterito Ladron de Amor – Ntra Sra Virgen de la Asunción
Bachelor Thief of Love – Our Lady, the Virgin of the Assumption *(SFT)*

Amarte Es Mi Delirio – Divino Sr. de Chocan F
To Love You Is My Delirium – Jesus of Chocan F *(Bus)*

Lima: VIEJO MI—QUERIDO VIEJO – *Amor a Diós*
My Old—My Beloved Old (What?) – Love to God. MFT

Solo Te Queda Mirarme – Jeronimo – Julia
You Only Stay to Admire Me – Geronimo – Julia *(Bus)*

Viveré en Tu Recuerdo – Santissima Trinidad
I'll Live in Your Memory – Holy Trinity *(MFT)*

Tu Sufres al Verme – Luigi / You Suffer when you See Me – Luigi *(MFT)*

Cusco: 4 Hnos Para Todo Los Corazones – Chofer Soltero – César – Siempre César.
Four Brothers for All Those Hearts! – Bachelor Driver – Caesar – Always Caesar.
A gasoline truck (garaged) with four brothers?

DINA
Regalame un Beso y Dime Adios!
671 GG
SPE MEX 1984

NOMBRES y COMPAÑIAS

Oaxaca: Hermínio Pérez Hernández – Servicio Particulár / Herminio Perez Hernandez – Private Service
Many trucks, like this one, carry designations of their owners on their doors.
Like dichos, they may be simple or elaborate. This owner used not only dichos, but also decals:
the eagle is very popular; the No Llevo with the picture is very suggestive,
as is the No Te Hagas and its bull with the large nose; and the other decal needs no translation!

INTRODUCTION

This Chapter presents the Latin drivers' approach to naming a private or company vehicle. The names which they use are interesting in themselves, and may be simply or elaborately painted on the front doors of the vehicle, usually a truck, somewhat as in the United States of America. Similarly, the painting of names of family members in various locations on trucks and cars and taxis is a common sight.

Vehicles and companies often share similar names:
> Brisas de las Cumbres / Breezes of the Hills (a bus); and
> La Cumbreña / The Hilly One (its company).

Names are so common on buses in Guatemala that, for all countries in this Chapter, only vehicles which are *NOT* buses have been identified. A few names could not be translated.

Oaxaca: MI DGE Caráy / My Good Ol' Caray! (My Large Tortoise Shell)
Caray usually denotes surprise, as in Hay! Que Caráy; this dicho appeared, in fancy lettering,
on the back of a shiny, well-cared-for, red PT with a couple of soft drink bottles on the bumper!

INTRODUCCIÓN

Este Capítulo presenta el medio que toma los choferes latinos para nombrar un vehículo privado o de una compañía. Los nombres que usan son interesantes en tre sí mismos y pueden ser pintados sencillamente o floridamente sobre las puertas de adelante de un vehículo, usualmente un camión, un poco como en los Estados Unidos de América. Semejantemente, es común ver los nombres de miembros de la familia pintados en varios lugares sobre camiones y vehículos particulares y taxis.

Los vehículos y las compañías frecuentemente reparten nombres similares:
Brisas de las Cumbres (el autobus) y La Cumbreña (la compañía)

Nombres sobre los autobuses en Guatemala son muy comunes y por ésto, por todos los países en este capítulo, solo los vehículos que *NO* son autobuses han sido identificados. Algunos de los nombres ne se pudieron traducir.

BOLIVIA

LA PAZ

Los Angeles / The Angels *(M-Bus)*   Oriental *(MFT)*
Pancho Villa   Magno / Alexander the Great *(M-Bus)*
San Felix *(SFT)*   San Miguel *(MFT)*
San Martin de Porres *(MFT)*   San Silvestre / Saint Sylvester
San Ysidro / Saint Ysidro *(M-Bus)*   Señor de Mayo / Christ of Mayo
Señor Tormenta / Mister Storm

La Paz: Minerito del Cajones / Source of Odds and Ends.
On an MFT in the Ourouáy Market

ECUADOR

OTAVALO

Don Alfonso *(MFT)*   Edison
Júlio César   Lolita *(PT)*
Mery (Mary?) *(MFT)*   Niño Berry *(front & back LFT)*
Santiaguito / Little Santiago *(PT)*

QUITO

Aladino / Aladdin *(MFT)*   Bachita
Blanquita *(SFT)*   Carlitos
Centinela del Norte / Sentinel of the North
Cristinita   Dieguito *(LFT)*
El Creís / Real Crazy *(Slang)*   Eduardito *(SFT)*
El Fujitivo *(SFT)*   El Fujitivo Samuray
El Graduado / The Graduate *(Movie)* *(LFT)*
El Idolo / The Idol   El Médico / "Doc" *(MFT)*
El Titanic   Faustito *(SFT)*
Jaimito Jr.   La Nave / The Ship *(LFT)*
Marco Vinicio *(SFT)*   Maria Lorena *(MFT)*

QUITO

Marquito *(Van)*

Mois / Moses

Niña Nancy *(SFT)*

Mi Rosita

Niña Katy *(SFT)*

Paulito *(SFT)*

Reino de Quito Coop / Kingdom of Quito Coöp

Simplemente Maria / Just Plain Maria *(MFT)*

Super Jet 40

The Blue Jeet

Tarqui (The Battle of Tarquí)

Vencedores de Pichincha / Victors at Pichincha

(The last battle fought for the independence of Ecuador; it followed the Battle of Tarquí)

GUATEMALA

ALMALONGA

Lidia

AMATITLÁN

Charras / (from Charro?)

Mirtala

ANTIGUA GUATEMALA

Brisas de las Cumbres / Breezes of the Hills *(bus of the La Cumbreña Bus Line)*

Camélia

DORITA – SOLEDAD *(mudflaps)*

El Marciano / The Martian

Carmañola

El Chiquitito / The Tiny One

Granizadas / Ices

Golondrina de las Cumbres / Hill Swallow *(La Cumbreña Bus Line)*

Jéssica

La Majolli

Los Trabajadores / The Workers

Maria Linda

Mirna Esperanza

Nuestros Amigos / Our Friends

Verde y Rojo / Green and Red

La Reina #3 *(handcart for produce)*

La Samaria / Samaria

Luz / Light

Mi Corazón / My Love

Ninfa / Nymph

Primarosa / First Rose

Viqui / Vicky

Quito: Sergio Santiago – Club Riber Olímpico – Comerciál Delgado.
Sergio Santiago *(owner, top front)* – Olympic River Club *(back body)* – Delgado Co.
Very typical South American trucks, generally *(SFT)*

CANTÉL

Helda

Solveralma

CHIMALTENANGO

Carmencita

Larita

Hilda Esperanza

COATEPÉQUE

Gaitan / Good for nothing, Jealous

Genova

Los Independientes / The Independents

ESQUINTLA

La Reina Esquintleca / Escuintla Queen

Tejida / Weaving, Woven

GUATEMALA

Adaza / Panic Grass

Alemana / German Lady

América

Ana Luisa

Belmont

Chica de Mi Barrio / (The) Cutie of My Neighborhood

Chinita / L'il Darlin' (Indian girl)

Cine de Utitlán / Movie Theater of Utitlán

Claudia Carolina

Conchita

Contreras

Consentida / Spoiled One (Pampered)

Dalila

Delta

Doña Cata / Lady Catherine

El Grande *(MFT)*

Ericka

Favorita / Favorite Lady

Gaviota / Sea Gull

Jardinera / Gardener Lady

Juanita

La Belleza / The Beauty

La Colegiala / College Girl

La Humilde / The Humble One

La Nena Mi Lupita / My Baby Lupita

La Patoja / Girl

La Pituja / The Goblin

La Reinita / The Little Queen

Lilian de Rosario

Lilian Karina

Lleny

Lorena Elizabeth

Luciferito *(Red PT)*

Macarena / Boastful Lady

Malagueña / Lady of Malaga

Marcos / Frames

Maria Concepción

Maria del Mar / Mary of the Sea

Marinita

Marta Luisa

MAYA--GRICELDA *(mudflaps)*

Micro Alas / Tiny Wings

Mensajera / Messenger

Mixta! / Half Breed

Monica

Monja / Nun

Muchachita / Little Kid (Girl)

Navas / Valleys

Niña Bonita / Little Beauty

Niña Colegiala / College Girl

Norma

GUATEMALA

Odett   Novia del Sheik / The Sheik's Girlfriend

Panameña / Panamanian Lady   Patty

Pequeña Lulu / Little Lulu   Primavera / Primrose

Quinmarin Nola   Rebuli

Reina de las Flores / Queen of Flowers   Roly *(Florid gothic script!)*

Rosita   Rubia / Blonde *(Yellow bus with red trim)*

Super Veliz / Super Valise   Suplente / Substitute

Tormenta / Storm, Misfortune   Tumbador / Drummer

Vicky

LAS APOSENTES
La Pequiñita / Little Lady

Guatemala: Chinita / L'il Darlin'.
Photograph of a moving bus taken through the windshield of a moving car,
this fuzzy photo still captures the spirit of the dicho.

LOS ENCUENTROS
San Andrés

MAZATENANGO

Mazate Cuvo / Hammer shaft? *(bus fringe)*   Olguita / Little Olga

MIXCO

Charro	Guadalupe
Linda Kelly	Masanita / Little Mass (Lightweight)
Santa Cruz	Santa Lucia

NAHUALÁ

Halcones / Falcons	Higueros / Fig Trees

PAJAPITA

Valiente / Valiant

PALÍN

Tormenta / Storm

POAQUÍL

Chumil *(PT)*	Romancito / Little Roman *(PT)*

QUETZALTENANGO

Carmela	Chacho (Ice Cream Cart)
Islanderia / Islander	Julianita
La Violeta (Ice Cream Cart)	Las Florecitas / The Little Flowers
Linda Chapinita / Beautiful Guatemalan (Chapin) Lady	
Maricelita	Ramirez
Rosa Linda / Beautiful Rose	Rosario
San Antonio	STOP–SI / Stop–Yes (Ice Cream)
Veronica	

RETALHULEU

Gramajo

SALCAJÁ

Esmeralda

SAN JUAN SUCHITEPÉQUEZ

Alma Muñeca / Soul of a Doll	La Bella / The Beauty
Marroquin / Moroccan	Velaszquez

SAN LUCAS SACATEPÉQUEZ

Favorita / Favorite Lady	Mary

TECPÁN

Chinita / Little Girl (Indian Sweetie)	Rubensito / Little Ruben

TOTONICAPÁN

Azucena / Lily; Amaryllis	Esperanza / Lady of Hope
Madera de los Angeles / Los Angeles Wood	

GUATEMALA

Bus Companies

ANTÍGUA GUATEMALA

California — Carmoñola
Carrillo / Cart — Concepción
Eureka 776 — Flór de Barrio / Flower of the Barrio
Flór de Calle / Flower of the Street — Flór de Mi Tierra / Flower of My Land
Franciscana — La Chinita / The Little Darling
La Cumbreña / The Hilly One
La Española / The Spanish Lady
La Mejor / The Best — La Reina / The Queen
La Reina Antigueña / The Antiguan Queen
La Miniatura / The Miniature — La Rencedora / ??
La Tuneca / The Tunisian
Maya Excélsior – La Preferida de Guatemala (bumper)
Microfé / Microfaith — Primarosa / First Rose
Reína Antigüeña — Reína del Unapu / Queen of Unapu
Samayoa — San Rafaél

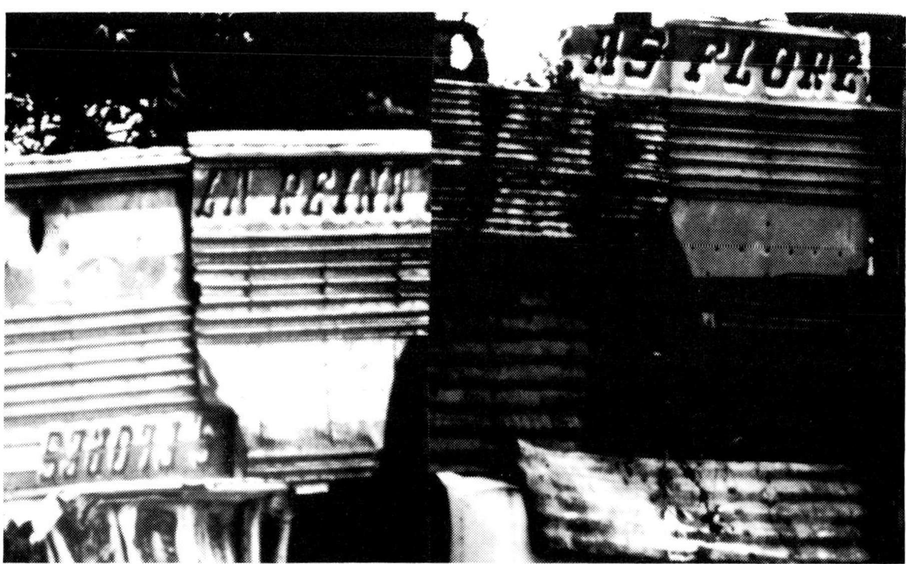

Mixco: Reina de las Flores / Queen of the Flowers
A large bus line, at the end, contributing to a fence of bus parts:
old buses never die, they just get fenced!

AYUTLA
Veloz Portán

CANTÉL
Carmelo   Suq

CHIMALTENANGO
La Veloz Poaquileña

GUATEMALA
Aurora   De Barrio / From the Barrio
De Mi Tierra / From My Land   Causa 57 / Cause 57
Cíudad Reál / Royal City *(Microbus)*
El Mensajero del Norte / The Messenger of the North
Flómitax   Flór de Barrio
Flór de Maria   Flór del Café / Coffee Flower
Flór de Mi Tierra – Gemelos / Flower of My Land – Twins
Fortaleza / Fortress   Fuente Del Norte / Fountain of the North
Gaviota / The Sea Gull   Humilde / Humble
La Camélia   La Cubanita / Little Cuban Lady
La Flór / The Flower   La Preferida / The Preferred One
La Orellana *(One bus also had Orellana-Orellana written on both bumpers)*
La Tacaná / The Miser, also the Volcano
Macarena   Malagueña
Marcos   Mensajera / Messenger
Mi Tierra / My Land (Guatemala)   Morena / Dark One *(with black bumpers)*
Motores Ifal   Muñeca / Doll
Norma   Paiz Hnos / Paiz Bros.
Preciosa / Precious Lady   Predilecta / Favorite Lady
Primavera / Spring   Princessita del Rio / Little River Princess
Reina de las Flores / Queen of the Flowers
Reina del Trópico – Queen of the Tropics
Risueña / The Smiling Lady   San Martineca / Lady from San Martin
Sonrisa / Smile

NAHUALÁ
Moreliana

PARRAMOS
Transportes Caprillo

PATZÚN
Flór de Mayo / May Flower

QUETZALTENANGO

Bartolenses   Mendez
Santa Fé / Holy Faith   Sula
Tecún Umán

RETALHULEU

Rutas de León / The Lion's Routes

SALCAJÁ

Esmeralda   Juveníl / Youthful
Micro Linda / Microbus Linda   San Gabriél

SAN LUCAS SACATEPÉQUEZ

Lux / Light   Orellana
Sumpanguera / Lady from Sumpango   Velóz Antigueña

TOTONICAPÁN

Reina Indiana / Indian Queen   Rutas Norato
Rutas Osorio   San Cristobal

MEXICO

ACAPULCO

Apache / Apache *(MFT)*   Coadília *(MFT)*
Ben Hur *(18-T)*   Caíga / Fallen One
Cheyene / Cheyenne (Indian) *(MFT)*   Claudia *(MFT)*
Cowboy *(handwritten 6 times on a bus)*   Doña Mico *(MFT)*
El Vikingo / The Viking *(MFT)*   Gran Noe / ? *(MFT)*
Israel *(MFT)*   Julugán *(18-T)*
Leña Verde / Green Wood *(MFT)*   Lilian / Lillian *(MFT)*
Maria Anita *(MFT)*   Maria Cruz *(PT)*
Micky *(MFT)*   Pedrín / Big Peter *(flatbed MFT)*
Rocky *(MFT)*   Rules / Roll Thou! (Vulgar) *(MFT)*
Santa Rosa *(MFT)*   Tacho (Nickname: Francisco) *(18-T)*
Xochitepec #² *(MFT)*

ACATLAN

Oscar Marisol *(SFT)*

AHUMADA

La Rosita / The Little Rose *(PT)*   Hungary / Hungarian *(18-T)*

AXIXINTLA

El Poblano / The Pueblan *(PT)*

BERMEJILLO
"Tony"

BUCERIAS

Gitano / Gypsy *(DT)* Gitano II / Gypsy No. II *(DT)*

CAMARGO

Chamaco / Urchin Pancho / Francisco nickname

CHIHUAHUA

Ché = Beto / *(Nicknames)* *(18-T)* Mezcalero / Mexcal Man *(18-T)*

CHILPANCINGO

Amaruza *(MFT)* Churrasco / Broiled Meat *(MFT)*
Cimmarón / Untamed *(MFT)* Correón / Big Strap *(18-T)*
Manvo *(MFT)* Pancho *(18-T)*
San Miguelito / Little Saint Michael *(MFT)*
Viva / Lively Wendy A/III / Wendy *(18-T)*

CIUDAD JUÁREZ

Cometa / Comet *(18-T)* El Chato / The snub-nosed
Hector – Jesús Jeny y Maria *(PT)*
La Cientifica / The Scientific *(MFT)* La Kinma / ?
Maira *(18-T)* Rocio *(PT)*
Naranjer"0"s / Orange Tree (with "0" being an Orange) *(LFT)*
"Side-Kick" *(PT)* The Angel *(MFT)*
The Rocker *(PT)* The Titanic

COMONFORT

El Yaqui (Yanqui?) *(DT)*

CRUZ DE HUANACÁXTLE

Potrillo / Young-Old One *(DT)*

CUAUTLA

Bufalo Bill I / Buffalo Bill No. I *(DT)* Danielito / Little Daniel *(MFT)*
Manutzi / ? *(MFT)* Pequeño Bolívar *(MFT)*
Rafito *(18-T)* Rosita / Little Rose *(MFT)*
San Ignacio V / St. Ignatius No. 5 *(MFT)*
Santa Fe † / Holy Faith (with slanted cross) *(DT)*

CUERNAVACA

Angelito / Little Angel *(MFT)*
Kendor III / Kendor 3 (*El Hombre del Tibet*, a hero of supernatural comics) *(MFT)*

ETLA
Tobruk *(MFT)*

FRESNILLO
Blanca –– Isabel *(18-T)*   Imelda *(18-T)*
Tinajero / Water Jar Man *(18-T)*

GOMEZ PALÁCIO
Avigeo *(LFT)*   El Rorro / Doll Baby

GUADALAJARA
Carnivalito *(MFT)*   Easy Rider *(18-T)*
Plaga / Plague *(MFT)*   The Fisherman *(18-T)*
Pachuco / El Paso (the city of El Paso; also a man with a jive costume and a special language) *(MFT)*

GUZMAN
El Gran Ari 4 *(LFT)*

Gomez Palacio: 29 – Super Star
Super Star is, clearly, a thoughtful Jesus Christ, as His likeness appears with "Super Star."
"29" is the bus number.

IGUALA

Barrientos / Sweepers *(MFT)*
Gargantua *(18-T)*
Monica *(tank truck)*
Tata Gildo III *(MFT)*

Becerro / Little Bull *(18-T)*
Goliat *(Pepsi-Cola truck)*
Papi *(MFT)*
Tauro / Taurus *(MFT)*

IXTAPAN DE LA SAL

Dalila *(MFT)*
"Zeuz" *(18-T)*
El Chicano *(MFT)*
Juve / ? Youth *(MFT)*
Pito / ? Francisco *(MFT)*
Tribilín / ? *(18-T)*

Mad Max *(PT)*
19––Rene––45 *(18-T)*
Jorge Antonio / George Anthony *(MFT)*
Mi Che *(18-T)*
Santander *(18-T)*

JILOTEPEC

El Texano *(MFT)*

Neto *(18-T)*

JIMENEZ

Adelita / Little Adela *(Adelitas were, however, the camp followers of the Mexican Revolution)* *(MFT)*

Bertha––Alicia II *(MFT)*
Candy *(18-T)*
Hebreo / Hebrew *(MFT)*
Libra 2° *(MFT)*

California *(18-T)*
EL 1° *(18-T)*
Hernandez 4° *(MFT)*
"Sultan" *(18-T)*

Tacón / Heel, or Large Taco! *(18-T)*

JUÁN ALDAMA

Almita / Little Alma *(LFT)*
La Tejana *(PT)*
Nautilus *(MFT)*

El Titico *(LFT)*
Jimenez *(18-T)*
Togo *(LFT)*

MÉTEPEC

"Bebe" / "Babe" *(DT)*

MEXICO D.F.

Berlin *(MFT)*

"Cowboy" *(18-T)*

OAXACA

Alex *(MFT)*
Anna –– Lilia H. –– Carmelita *(SFT)*
Aracely *(very common; apopears also as ARACELI; Farm and PTs)*
Chabelo 52 *(18-T)*
Chemita II / ? *(MFT)*
Chiquilita / Little Cutie
Cóquis *(nickname for Socorro)* *(PT)*

Ana Laura
Chayito *(MFT)*
Cheto
Claudia
Coquito / Little Socorro

Izucar de Matamoros: Nazareth – Javiercito / Nazareth – Little Xavier.
A large farm truck with sunsets (or sunrises) and horses, both on the front bumper and the mudflaps.

OAXACA

Cristo del Valle / Christ of the Valley (of Oaxaca)

Damiancito / Little Damian *(MFT)*	Dolores *(PT)*
Edith *(MFT)*	El Canario / The Canary
Ebenezer	Edgar Ulises *(PT)*
El Bismarck *(MFT)*	"El General"
El Ché / ? *(MFT)*	Emperador / Emperor
Érika *(MFT)*	Felino / Feline *(MFT)*
Florecita	Getsemani / Gethsemane *(PT)*
Green Mary *(MFT with bright green cab)*	Jessica *(18-T)*
Jesús Manuél *(MFT)*	Jhonny *(MFT)*
Judas *(18-T)*	Julio Cesár
Juguete Caro / Expensive Toy *(LFT)*	Karla Marisól *(MFT)*
La Enena / ? *(PT)*	Lalín *(PT)*

La Niña Morena / The Dark-skinned Girl

Laurita *(PT)*	Leo / Leo *(MFT)*
Long Beach *(MFT)*	Mahoma / ?

Maquinita 501––Anita / Little Machine 501 *(MFT)*

Maria – José *(MFT)*	Mario Alberto *(PT)*
Mary––Toña *(PT)*	Marysol *(SFT)*
Miguelón / Big Mike *(MFT)*	Moïses / Moses
Mundín / ? *(MFT)*	Nidia Soldeva *(MFT)*
Nilita / Little Nila *(SFT)*	Ofelia / Ophelia *(PT)*
Omar *(PT)*	Panchita / Little Francesca *(MFT)*

Olguita ––La Chatita / Little Olga ––Little Pug-Nose *(PT)*
Panchita––Teresita / Little Francisca and Little Teresa *(SFT)*

Pancho Villa
Pegaso / Pegasus
Raffles *(LFT)*
Rocín *(18-T)*
San Sebastián *(MFT)*
Santa Lucia *(MFT)*
Silvita / Little Sylvia *(PT)*
Sn Francisco *(MFT)*
Sn Salvador *(MFT)*
Sto Domingo *(PT)*
Super Bee *(PT)*
Tropical del Valle / A Tropical of the Valley *(of Oaxaca; with musical notes!) (PT)*
Tunante / Truant, Rake
Vernoica *(PT)*
Virgencita Juquila / Little Virgin of Juquila *(MFT)*

Paty
Pilar *(PT)*
Raulito / Little Raul
Salinera / Salt Carrier *(MFT)*
Santa Julia *(PT)*
Sergio-Veronica *(PT)*
"Siboney"
Sn José *(PT)*
Solitário / Bachelor *(flatbed MFT)*
Super Agua / Super Water *(waterbottle truck)*
The Renegade *(VW 'Bug')*
Velia *(MFT)*
Vizuriky *(MFT)*

Zeus / Jove

PALO BLANCO
"Zapata" *(SFT)*

PUEBLA

Kalman *(MFT)*
Tarragona / Tarragon *(MFT)*

"Kennedy" *(MFT)*
Pepe – Pepe *(MFT)*

PUERTO VALLARTA
"Monica" *(SFT)*

QUARENTA Y CINCO

Bartolomeo *(MFT)*
Love 69 *(The 69 scratched into the front bumper paint) (MFT)*

QUERÉTERO

Hercules I *(MFT)*
Richard *(MFT)*
El Tahur / The Gambler *(MFT)*

SAN CRISTOBAL DE LAS CASAS

Alain *(PT)*
Chamo / Shorthair *(MFT)*
Inosente *(MFT)*
Resentor / Resenter *(MFT)*
San Cristobal *(MFT)*

Ana Laura *(PT)*
Cimmarón / Wild One *(LFT)*
La Chilindrina / The Trifle *(MFT)*
Maria del Carmen *(PT)*
Santa Catarina *(MFT)*

SAN CRISTOBAL DE LAS CASAS

Sara – Patricia *(MFT)*
Soraya *(MFT)*
Tio Luis / Uncle Louis *(PT)*

SAN GABRIEL CHILÁC

Melina *(SFT)*   Omarcito / Little Omar

SAN JUAN DE LA PAZ

El Gutierrez *(MFT)*   "Wicho" *(MFT)*

SAN LUIS POTOSÍ

Cherokee *(MFT)*   Rambo / ? *(MFT)*

SANTA MARIA DEL RIO

Toro *(DT)*   Poncho 1° *(DT)*   "21 Negro" *(MFT)*

SAUCILLO

Joker / Comodín *(PT)*

TAXCO

Beatris y Oliva *(PT)*   Convoy *(18-T)*
Cuahtemoc *(MFT)*   Dartagnan (Gothic) *(LFT)*
Edgar el Chicano   El Consentido / The Pampered One
El Globo / The Balloon   El Gordo / Fatty *(VW 'Bug' Taxi)*
El Taptín *(MFT)*   El Vagabundo / Vagabond *(VW 'Bug' Taxi)*
Jumilero & Flor Moreno *(the latter could well refer to the driver!) (MFT)*
Juquita *(Ore Truck 18-T)*   La Chiquiríquis / Teeny-Tiny One *(LFT)*
La Güera / The Blonde *(Superior beer truck)*   La Niña *(SFT) (PT)*
Letitia *(18-T)*   Miguelito / Little Miguel *(MFT)*
Mocosita / Brat *(VW Bug Taxi)*   Papi / Pappy *(MFT)*
Salinero / Salt Man *(18-T)*   Vaquero / Cowboy *(VW Bug Taxi)*
Tutis / Tutties *(from 'Tutia,' Tutty, or zinc oxide residues?) (MFT)*

*Oaxaca: * Lupita * – Monte Alban Oax. Little Guadalupe – Monte Alban, Oaxaca.*
on the camper shell is a painting of Monte Alban, one of the most famous ruins in Mexico.
On the door is a decal of Jiminy Cricket with an ice cream cone! (PT)

Oaxaca: Moshe Dayán
It is common to see names of international flavor painted on the sides of buses.

TECOMAVACA
El Teo Titeco / The Man from Teotitán *(SFT)*

TEHUACÁN
Arturito / Little Arthur *(FT)*   Chayin Primero *(MFT)*
Chelita / Little Coin *(MFT)*   Chepita *(SFT)*
El Mago / The Magician *(18-T)*   Gamfa *(MFT)*
Jeque / Old Man *(18-T)*   Rumor *(MFT)*   Lorena *(MFT)*

TIERRA COLORADA
Erick *(MFT)*   Jibarito / Little Annoyer *(18-T)*
Maria – Anita *(MFT)*   Monarca

TOLUCA
Cancer

TUXPAN
Juan Pablo II *(18-T)*   Mi Generál *(18-T)*
Mi Tormento *(18-T)*

TUXTLA GUTIERREZ
Cositia   San Diegito / Little San Diego
Villa Flores / Flower Villa   Villa Reál / Royal Villa

YAÚTEPEC
Pacifico II *(SFT)*   Yellow Submarine *(18-T)*

YERMO
Alicia's *(18-T)*

ZACATECAS
Stone *(gravel-carrying 18-T)*   Togo *(LFT)*   "Yusi" *(18-T)*

MEXICO
Companies

GOMEZ PALACIO
Transportes 13 de Marzo *(Bus line)*

SAN CRISTOBAL DE LAS CASAS
Mercado–Párque Centrál –Panteón–San Felipe y Viceversa *(Bus line)*

PANAMA

PANAMA
Baretta *(Painting of him and parrot, back door)*
El Caminante de Atalaya / The Atalaya Traveller *(PT)*
El Dinamico / The Dynamic   El Famoso / The Famous
El Guapo / The Handsome   El Increíble / The Incredible
El Guaymi / Panamanian Indian *(painting, back door)*
El Mago del Oriente / The Wizard of the East
(painting, Samurai-like figure in Japanese scene; back door)
El Nivelador / The Leveller   El Rey / The King *(side door; old PT)*
El Tesoro / The Treasure   General MacArthur *(DT)*
Express Don Chico / Mr. Little's Express Bus

Taxco: El Ranchito / The Little Ranch.
This little hot food cart (Ranchito) stands near the main, south entrance to the city.
The Brahma bull chewing the wisp of straw is intended, perhaps, to inspire throughts of freshness.
There is also a decorative hog on the right side. Some informal electrical wiring may also be seen!

Mister Tile––La Sensación / Mr. Tile––The Sensation!
Lucho *(nickname)*   Mario Augusto
Mi Tio Porfírio / My Uncle Profírio *(M-Bus)*
Panamá Bendita / Blessed Panama *(painting, flags, canal, boats, forest; very fancy!)*
Pony Exprez
Rita––Creo en Diós / Rita––I Believe in God

Sergio Tiburón / Sergio (the) Shark)
Un Caballero de Natá––Cacíque Nata / Gentleman of Nata––Nata Chief
Vigilante / Vigilante   …WHEN… / Cuando

PERU

CUSCO

Ben Hur   Luchin *(SFT)*
Robert––Milton *(MFT)*   Rony *(Taxi)*
Tony Baretta   Walter *(SFT)*
William III *(MFT)*   Yauqueño *(man from Yauca) (MFT)*

LIMA

Angelita *(MFT)*   Californía *(MFT)*
Ballon Arnao / Arnold's Balloon   Carlitos *(SFT)*
Cesaro *(LFT)*   César––Saúl *(LFT)*
Cinturón Negro / Black Belt *(2 MFTs)*   Don Adrián *(MFT)*
Don Marcelino N°2 *(MFT)*   Don Felipe – Mi Consuelo *(SFT)*
El Astro / The Star   El Cholo / Darliing *(SFT)*
El Diamante Negro / The Black Diamond *(The Driver?) (MFT)*
El Señor de Chilca / Christ of Chilca   El Pionero / The Pioneer *(MFT)*
Francia / France *(MFT)*   Gitano / Gypsy *(MFT)*
Gitano / Gypsy *(MFT)*   Josecito – Lil' Joe *(MFT)*
José António N°2 *(SFT)*   Katy N°4 *(MFT)*
Lima Limón *(A play on Lima, the city, and our Lemon,
and Limón, a large Lima, a Lime, or the 'Great City of Lima'!) (MFT)*

*Oaxaca: El Kid Mixteco – "Jeny" – Que Murmuren – lo Que Fuimos No Se Olvide.
The Mixtec Kid – Jenny – May They Say that What We Have Done Will Not Be Forgotten.
Que Murmuren was painted on body above the rest of the dicho on the spare tire. (MFT)*

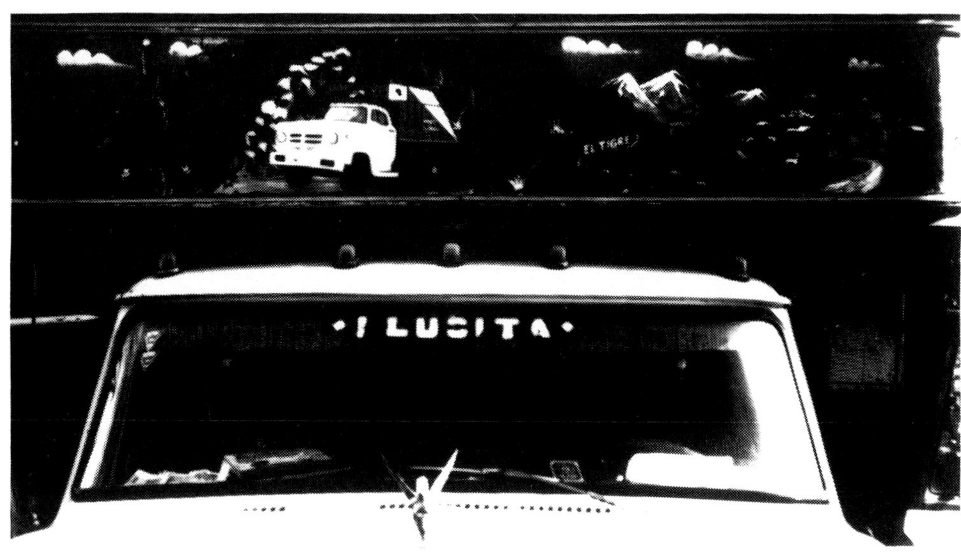

LIMA

Mahetigo *(The surname of five brothers)* (Bus)

Marina Violeta – Sr. de Locumba *(MFT)* Mi Sandra / My Sandra

Mi San Juanito *(MFT)* Mi Zambito / My Little Blackie *(MFT)*

Moïses / Moses Montaña / Mountain *(LFT)*

Papi / Papa *(MFT)* Rambo / ?

Ringo (Starr) *(MFT)* San Jacinto *(SFT)*

San Cristobal Caminante / Saint Christopher, The Traveller *(18-T)*

San Juanito *(MFT)* San Lorenzo *(LFT)*

(San) Luis *(sign being painted on front, only the Luis was finished)* *(MFT)*

Siete Lagunas / Seven Lagoons (Lakes) *(MFT)*

Toño / Antonio (Tony) *(SFT)*

Lima: Lusita / El Tigre
A well-painted mural on the front of the body of an SFT.
The significance of El Tigre is not known. Note also the small vicuña.

Dichos con
REFRANES

Cuautla: Un hogar sin SANCHO es como un JARDIN sin flores – CUPIDO – Travieso – Atlatlahucar
A house without Sancho is like a garden with flowers – Cupid (with a heart) – Naughty –
Man from Atlatlahuca
Sancho is a character in Mexico who plays with a wife while her husband is at work! (LFT)

INTRODUCTION

Proverbs, or Refranes, are important to every culture, and the Latin Americans are no exception. Some are very humorous and international:

En Boca Cerrada No Entran Moscas / No Flies Enter a Closed Mouth

Some are equivalents to other proverbs in the English language, though the equivalency may not immediately be obvious:

Andando de Cacería Cualquiér Lagartija es Bueno

Literally: When you are hunting, any old lizard will do. In English, this is:

Beggars can't be choosers

I have included a special section on proverbs, as they are so telling a reflection of a society's way of thinking, and because it takes a lot of effort to paint a whole *refran* on the bumper of a truck or a bus!

Panamá: Mas vale cliente en mano que cien huyendo – El Salta Monte II
A Client at hand is worth a hundred running away – The Grasshopper No. 2. (Large Van)

INTRODUCCIÓN

Los refranes son importantes para todas las culturas y los Latino-americanos no son excepción. Algunos son muy humorísticas e internacionales:

En Boca Cerrada No Entran Moscas.

Algunos son equivalentes a otros refranes de nuestra lengua. Inglés, aunque la equivalencia no se pueda notar inmediatamente:

Andando de Cacería Cualquier Lagartija es Bueno

En Inglés, es   Beggars Can't Be Choosers.

He incluido una sección especial sobre refranes, como son tan reveladores del pensamiento de una sociedad y porque toma mucho esfuerzo pintar un refran entero sobre el contrachoque de un camión o de un autobus!

BRAZIL

RIO DE JANEIRO
Quen Ama as Rosas Sofre os Espinhos
Whoever Loves Roses must put up with the Thorns (MFT)

ECUADOR

OTAVALO
La Envidia Te Mata / Jealousy Will Be the Death of You (SFT)

QUITO
La Envidia Te Mata, Hijo / Envy Will Kill You, Son
(Written in cut up adhesive tape on back window) (Bus)

Trabaja y No Envidias / If You Work You Will Not Be Envious *(vehicles!)*

En la Casa de Ahorcado no Hay Que Mentar la Soga
In the House of the Hanged, One Does Not Mention the Rope (MFT)

Pobre pero Ondrado *[*Honrado*]* / (Be a) Poor Man but Honorable (SFT)

Peór Es Nada / Nothing Can Be Worse
(particularly poignant, this was painted on a very, very, very old car)

Mas Vale Aquí Corrió Que Aquí Morió
It is Better to have Run Here than to have Died Here
(usually applied to wild drivers, to encourage them to be cautious) (SFT)

GUATEMALA

ANTÍGUA GUATEMALA
Hacer Bién a Villanos es Echár Água en el Mar
To Be Good to Villains in Like Throwing Water into the Ocean (MFT)

En Casa de Herrero, Cuchillo de Palo
There are Only Wooden Spoons in the Blacksmith's House (MFT)

Quién Siembra Vientos Recoge Tempestadas
He Who Sows Winds, Reaps Tempests (MFT)

En Boca Cerrada no Entran Moscas / No Flies Enter a Closed Mouth (Bus)

Dádivas Quebrantan Piedras / Gifts (can) Break Stones (Bus)

Al Enemigo Que Huye, Puente de Plata
To an Enemy Who Flees, a Bridge of Silver (Bus)

Más Vale Ser Cabeza de Ratón que Cola de León
It is Better to be the Head of a Rat than the Tail of a Lion *(PT)*

El Que Hace Para Buiro Rehuznando Muere
He Who is Born Refusing Polish Dies *(Bus)*

MAS VALE TARDE –– QUE NUNCA / Better Late Than Never *(mudflaps SFT)*

Vino Mujér y Tabaco Dejan al Ombre Bién Flaco
Wine, Women and Tobacco Leave a Man very Weak (frail, dejected, lazy) *(Bus)*

MEXICO

ACAPULCO
Andando de Cacería Cualquiér Lagartija es Bueno
When You are Hunting, Any Old Lizard Will Do *(PT delivering meat)*

CUERNAVACA
Las Noches Las Haga Dias / The Nights Make the Days *(MFT)*

MÉXICO D.F.
Cuentas Cabales Hacen Buenas Amistades
Correct Accounts Make Good Friendships *(PT)*

OAXACA
Dejad Que Los Perros Ladren Que Vamos Cabalgando
Let The Dogs Bark All They Want, for We Are on Horses *(Tall MFT)*

Del Dicho al Hecho Hay Gran Trecho
From Saying to Doing is a Long Way *(LFT)*

TEHUACÁN
El Sabio no Discute con el Necio / The Wise Discuss not with the Foolish *(SFT)*

PANAMA

PANAMÁ
Vive y Deje Vivir / Live and Let Live *(M-Bus)*

En Esta Vida Lo Mejor Es Callar / In This Life it is Best to Hold Your Tongue
(with back door painting of a sweet lady) *(Bus)*

No Hay Atajo Sin Trabajo – Virgen del Carmen – Miguelito
There is No Shortcut Without Work – Virgin of Carmen – Little Mike *(SFT)*

Vive Tu Vida y Deja Vivir / Lead Your (own) Life and Let (others) Live (Theirs)
(small car)

Camina y Prende el Fogón / Go Out and Make a Good Fire
(In the sense of Get Busy and Cook My Dinner!) (PT)

PERU

CUSCO
Trabaja y No Envidies – Jessy / Work and Don't Be Envious – Jessie *(MFT)*

LIMA
No Se Ganá pero se Goza / Only What is Earned is Enjoyed *(Taxi Van)*

Oaxaca: "Caminante no Hay Camino Se Hace Camino al ANDAR."
The Traveller Has Only the Road which Is Made by Going. (SFT)

EL TRAVIESO
SB 6613
82 PUE MEX 83

Almalongo: Soy Hijo del Rey. / I'm the Son of the King.
This owner of a Small Farm Truck certainly liked his decorations and accessories.
It was parked by the side of the road, freshly wet from an Easter shower.

INTRODUCTION

The humor of a country is an index to its soul. In this chapter, a motley group of *dichos* has been assembled: the dominant themes of these *dichos* are jokes (outwardly or inwardly directed), and egoisms (professions of magnificence or of imperfection), or simply recognitions of human frailty.

There appear to be no national differences, just a universal outpouring of the ego of mankind. Occasionally, a little advertising creeps in:

Estoy Muy Linda "Visitame" – Posada de Los Castillo

I am Very Beautiful, Visit Me – The Inn of The Castillos.

In Mexico, American words are used with more frequency than other countries, especially in proximity to our mutual frontier. Yet, they appear everywhere.

Oaxaca: Armandín – El Travieso – Perro Callejero / Big Armando – Naughty One – Street Dog
(with pictures of a dog tugging at a bikini bottom!) (LFT)

INTRODUCCIÓN

El humor de un país es el indicio de su alma. En este capítulo, un grupo diverso de "dichos" ha sido juntado: los temas dominantes de estos dichos son chistes (dirigidos exteriormente o interiormente), egoísmos (profesiones de grandeza o de imperfección), o simplemente el reconocimiento de la debilidad humana.

No aparece que haya diferencia nacional, sólo un chorro universal del egoísmo del género humano. Ocasionalmente, un poco de propaganda está escondida, como:

Estoy Muy Linda "Visítame" – Posada de los Castillo.

En México, palabras americanas se usan con más frecuencia que en los otros países, especialmente en proximidad a nuestra frontera mutua. Sin embargo, aparecen por todas partes.

BOLIVIA

LA PAZ
El Invincible / The Invincible *(Bus)*

ECUADOR

OTAVALO
El Terible Bolito / The Terrific Drunkard *(Bus)*
Super Ford / Super Ford *(Bus)*
El Quitarán de Allí / The Super Macho *(MFT)*

Vengo pero sin Chismes / Here I Am – without Gossip *(MFT)*

QUITO
La Poderosa / The Powerful One *(small (PT)*
Super Freno / Super Brake(r) *(very old (PT)*

No Soy Dólar––per Subo / I'm Not the Dollar––but I Rise! *(MFT)*

Me Siento––109cito / I Feel––Renewed! *(MFT)*

El Verdadero Ejecutivo / The True Executive *(Bus)*

Siempre––Caballero––Chico de Oro / Always––a Gentleman––The Golden Kid
(LFT)

Caballero en el Camino / Cavalier of the Highway *(LFT)*

Transportamos Oro Negro / We transport Black Gold *(petroleum truck)*

No Me Sigas por que Estoy Perdido / Don't Follow Me––I'm Lost! *(MFT) (SFT)*

GUATEMALA

ANTÍGUA GUATEMALA
Lo Cóaster / The Coaster *(MFT)*

Llegarón Los Preferidos / The Preferred Ones Have Arrived
(Bus of the Maya Excelsior Line)

La Mujer Biónica – Abusadora / The Bionic Woman – The Abuser!
(Mudflaps and back, respectively of Risueña Line bus)

Los Borachos Son Gente Decente / Drunks Are Decent People *(Bus)*

Haz Mal y Guardatelo / Do Bad (Things), and Watch Out! *(Bus)*

Cuide Bien su Vehícula y Sonria / Take Good Care of your Vehicle and Smile
(Bus)

GUATEMALA
El Marcianito / The Little Martian *(PT)*
El Marciano / The Martian *(MFT)*
El Grande / The Big One *(SFT)*
Cosita Dulce / Sweet Thing *(Bus)*
Pequeño Orguillosa / Small, Proud One *(Bus)*
La Nave del Destino / The Ship of Destiny *(PT)*
Rosa La Rumo Rosa / Rosy the Gossip *(Bus)*
Caballero Audáz / Bold Gentleman *(MFT)*
La Humilde / The Humble *(Bus)*
Que Culpa Tengo Yo / How I Am to Blame! *(Bus)*

El Látigo del Sur / The Whip of the South *(Red LFT)*

Ricardo Corazón de León / Richard the Lion-Hearted *(MFT)*

La Silla Eléctrica / The Electric Chair *(panel truck)*

La Pese a Quien Le Pese / He Gives Her the Grief She Gives Him *(MFT)*

Soy Como Quiero Ser / I Am as I Would Like To Be *(MFT)*

Que Manero de Perder / What a Way to Lose! *(Bus)*

Algún Dia Seré Colocha / Someday I Will /not/ Be Messed Up *(Bus)*

Ay Tatita Ayúdame / Oh, Grandma, Help Me! *(car)*

Hay Papito No Corres Mucho / Papito No Corras Mucho
Oh, Grampa, You Don't Run Around Much *(trucks and buses)*

Cuidado Frenes de "Aire" / Caution, Air Brakes
(why this warning was so emphatic is not clear) (Bus)

Parecidas pero No Iguales / Similar, but not Equals *(Bus)*

Guatemala: XVII – HITLER – XVII
The reason for the name and numbers of the large, black Mercedes Benz farm truck is a mystery.
I have seen three, with different numbers. No driver was available to question.

QUETZALTENANGO
Principe Azúl / Blue Prince *(Blue LFT)*
El Andarriego / The Traveller *(LFT)*

SAN JUAN SUCHITEPÉQUEZ
TUS DESPRECIOS – ME DAN RISAS / Your Scorn Makes Me Laugh
(Mudflaps, (MFT)

ZUNÍL
Principe Inolvidable / Unforgettable Prince *(MFT)*

Coloso de los Altos / Colossus of the Heights *(MFT)*

MEXICO

ACAPULCO
El Juguéte Caro / The Expensive Toy *(MFT)*
El Sério / The Serious One *(MFT)*
El Canalla / The Rabble *(18-T)*
Aventurero / Adventurer *(MFT)*
Rey Sin Palácio / King without a Palace *(18-T)*
Mi Último Fracazo / My Ultimate Downfall *(Bus)*
"Rolling" – No Defense *(18-T and an 18-T Tank)*
Yo Nunca Muero / I (Will) Never Die *(SFT)*

El Vigilano / The Vigilant
(Vigilante is more usual; may be villano and vigilante!) (MFT)

El Conquistadór de Mongólia / The Conqueror of Mongolia *(Bus)*

Pópeye el Rey del Mar / Popeye, The King of the Sea
(SFT with a tarpaulin, contents unknown)

ACATLÁN
El Duende / The Hobgoblin
(has gold teeth and always smokes a cigar; in Mexico, refers also to a person's inner spirit) (MFT)

Medio ½ Traviezo / Half ½ Naughty! *(SFT)*

ACULCO
Once Hermanos / Eleven Brothers *(LFT)*
El Mandarin / The Mandarin *(orange LFT)*
La Uva Alegre / The Happy Grape *(green SFT)*
El Chico / The Little One *(red MFT)*

卐 Pirata 卐 / Pirate (with 2 swastikas!) *(red LFT)*

Oaxaca: Ya Yego (Llegó) Tu Viejo / Your Old Man Has Arrived ! (SFT)

BERMEJILLO
Hermano Loquio / Lunatic Brother (LFT)

CAMARGO
Errante / Errant (18-T)

CHIAPA DE CORSO
A Llego el Ausente / Here Comes the One Who was Far Away (MFT)

CHIHUAHUA
GATOR – "Mr. Fisk" (18-T from the city of Chihuahua)

El Rumbo Es Michoacán / The 'New Wave' Is Michoacán (LFT)

CHILPANCINGO
Cíudad Bravos / City of Angry Men (MFT)
Travieso / Restless (Mischievous) (MFT)
El Mitotero III / The Jolly III (MFT)
Edgar el Chicano / Edgar, the Chicano (MFT)
Orange 10 (orange-painted LFT)

CIUDAD JUÁREZ
Me Ven y Sufren / They See Me and Suffer! (station wagon)

Apenitas / Lots of trouble (affectionate) (MFT)

SIGALE DANDO / Back Off!
(The Mexican version with the little pirate waving two guns) (MFT)

"Sonny" *(PT)*
They See Me and Suffer! *(Stationwagon)*

Catch Me If You Can / Alcanceme Si Puede *(neatly done Texas car)*

Piél Canela / Cinnamon Skin *('exquisite') (livid green 18-T)*

El Chihuáhua / The Chihuahuan *(18-T)*
Emperadór / Emperor *(bold script) (18-T)*

CRUZ DE HUANACÁXTLE
Cruel Destiny! *(on a Tank truck with a flat tire!)*

"Ranchero" / Rancher *(Jeep CJ)*

No dicho: Picture of swimming sharks on both sides *(SFT)*

CUAUTLA
El 7 * Vidas / The Seven Lives *(* is a sun drawing) (MFT)*

Varron de Dolores / Man of Sorrows *(MFT)*

CUENCAMÉ
Caminante / Travelling *(on foot!) (18-T)*

CUERNAVACA
¿Soy La Chistosa? / I'm the Funny One? *(PT)*
Sombrero Rojo / Red Sombrero *(MFT)*
El Popa / The Prosperous One / *(MFT)*

Izucar de Matamoros: Amigo Soy de los Hombres y de las Mujeres ni Hablar
I Am a Friend to Men, to Say Nothing about Women! (SFT)

CUILAPAN
Payasito / Little Clown (MFT)

EL TREINTA
Falsa Ilusio / False Illusion (MFT)

ETLA
Commandante Cero / Commander Zero (MFT)

FRESNILLO
El Pionero / The Pioneer (18-T)

GOMEZ PALACIO
Se Busca / Takes Care of -Self (Him? Her? Its?) (MFT)

El Rapido / The Rapid One (18-T)
El Salvaje / The Savage (LFT)
Haber Si Puedo / I'll Have it if I Can! (LFT)
La Fuga de Rojo / The Red Flight (Red DT)

GUANAJUATO
Chicos Malos / Little Bad Ones (SFT)

GUZMAN
Cacahuatero / Peanut Man (LFT)

IGUALA
Es Cosa Mia / It's My Thing (MFT)
El Intocable / Untouchable One (MFT)
Se Ve Facil / It's Easy to See (red MFT)
Toro ..y Tú / The Bull – and You! (18-T)

Horizonte – 2000 / Horizon: 2000 (My goal: 2000AD) (MFT)

Paco Mio / My Paco (probably from Pacos, silver ores containing iron)
(18-T carrying iron reinforcement rods; not known if driver's name is Francisco!)

El Gorrión y Yo / The Sparrow and I (with musical notes on the bumper)
(18-T with laughing driver!)

Becerro / The Calf (presumably a young bull!) (18-T)
El Chocante / The Provocative One (18-T)

IRAPUÁTO / Popeye El Marino III / Popeye the Sailor Man No. 3 (SFT)

IXTAPAN DE LA SAL
Culpable Soy / I'm Culpable (LFT)
El Tirantes / The Suspenders (MFT)
No Soy Monedita de Oro / I'm Not a Little Coin of Gold (DT)

La Muerocita / The Little Dead One (the truck?) *(SFT)*

IZUCAR DE MATAMOROS
Sigamos Pecando / We Go on Sinning *(LFT)*
Yo Pecador / I Am a Sinner! *(LFT)*
Jinete Nocturno / Night Rider *(18-T)*

El Pasito Tránsito / One which Goes Slowly (and holds up a lot of traffic) *(MFT)*

Baron Rojo 2° / The Red Baron No. 2 *(SFT)*

Ya Llego el Poblanito / Here Comes the Pueblan *(SFT)*

JIMÉNEZ
Soy de Suerto / I'm in Luck *(MFT)*
El Vaquero 1† / The Cowboy No. 1 *(MFT)*
Mejorado / Bettered *(MFT)*

Primer Placer al Ser / First, the Pleasure of Being! *(18-T)*

JUÁN ALDAMA
El Heröe / The Hero *(An MFT accompanying a group of marathoners carrying a lighted torch)*

Oaxaca:
La Veracruzana – Llegó Simon Blanco / The Lady from Veracruz – Simon Blanco has Arrived.
In the Oaxaca Fruit and Vegetable Market is a 'bay' with this elaborate over-door painting of an
MFT and a papaya plantation. The truck has, on its cab, over the windshield, the dicho:
Llegó Simon Blanco, the owner of the first La Veracruzana company fruit truck!

MÉXICO DF
Somos Diferente / We are different *(MFT)*

No Corras No Seas / (If) You Don't Run, You Won't Make It *(MFT)*

The Destroyer *(red (SFT)*

MITLA
Cowboys *(18-T)*

MORELIA
A Pesar de Todo / In Spite of Everything *(LFT)*

Soy el Andaliego / I'm the Wanderer *(Bus)*

MOROLEÓN
Juán el Pecadór / John the Sinner *(MFT)*

OAXACA
Salinero / Salt Shaker *(18-T carrying salt)*
Jumal––El Rebelde / Jumal––The Rebel *(PT)*
La Reina / The Queen *(Bus)*
Cuatro Lágrimas / Four Tears *(Bus)*
El Alas de Oro / One with Gold Wings *(MFT)*

El Mos Tachón / The Big Mustache *(MFT)*
El Titanic / The Titan *(The Titanic?) (MFT)*
The Renegade / El Renegado *(white VW Bug)*

Oaxaca: Se Solicita – El Consiente / "We" Are Soliciting – Someone of Sound Mind.
This MFT was exceptionally neat, with metallic paint.
Yet, scratched into the paint next to this decal were the misspelled words for El Consciente.

Orad Sin Cesár / Pray Without Cease (PT)
La Consentida / The Pampered One (SFT)

El Chico Temido / The Little Dread One (MFT)
Principe Azul / Blue Prince (MFT)
Poeta – Campesino / Poet – Farmer (Bus)
El Mostachon / The Grand Mustache (MFT)
Indomable / Indomitable (MFT)

Terrible / (The) Terrible One (MFT)
Chamaca / Little Girl (on a huge red DT)
El Monarca––"Wuendy" – The Monarch––Wendy (Bus)
Nube Roja / Red Cloud (PT)
ESCLAVO / Slave (in large letters) (LFT)

Oye Gorda / Listen Here, Fatty (VW Bug)

Mala Cara / Ugly Face (makes faces; untrustworthy) (MFT)

El Sósio de Siléncio / The Companion of Silence (MFT)

Los Tres Consejos / The Three Words of Advice (MFT)

El Palomo / The Cock-Pigeon (worthless fellow) (MFT)

Perséguidor / The Persecutor (pursuer, molestor) (Bus)

¡No Que No! – Se Los Dije / Absolutely No! – I Told Them (MFT)

El Agentes Viajero / The Travel(ling) Salesmen) (Agents; assumes viajero to be traveler.
Could be a pun on viejo, 'old') (LFT) (Another SFT had El Ajente Viajero. Can't get it right!)

El Coyote de Neza Neza (football team) (MFT)

Maneje Con Cortesia – Guarde (Guarda) Su Distancia
Drive With Courtesy and Keep Your Distance (very frequent) (trucks & buses)

¡Cuadado! Power ¿Lobo? / Caution! Power Wolf? (PT)

El Extra Terrestre / The Extra-terrestrial (MFT)

Todo Por Nada / Everything (is) For Nothing (FT & DT)

La Nave Del Futuro / The Wave of the Future (Bus)

Caballero / Callejero / Gentleman – Wastrel (flatbed (MFT)

Leña Verde / Green Wood (MFT with green chicken crates

El Amigo del Pueblo / The Friend of the City (MFT)

La . Mano . Padrino / The Godfather's Hand
(The periods are probably decorative) (panel truck)

Mi Consentido / My Pampered One (very clean, shiny well-cared-for MFT)

Visite Tlachichula / Visit Tlachichula (spare tire, MFT)

Oaxaca: Hands Up / Manos Arriba
One of the occasional dichos in English, this one with two painted hearts and
'Puebla City' scratched crudely in the bumper's paint.
The intent remains unknown as no driver was near at the new market in Oaxaca. (MFT)

OAXACA

Diós Mi Diente / May God Keep My Tooth! (Adiós is implied, as in 'So Long, Tooth,'
as well as A Diós, or a request to God to preserve the tooth) *(MFT)*

Aquí Viene Tu Papa / Here Comes Your Papa (Papa also means Pope) *(Bus)*

¿Será Por Eso? / It (life) Will Be for all This?
(on the back of a flatbed brick truck)

El Rebelde / The Rebel
(It is unusual to see a dicho on a market pickup truck 'for hire') *(PT)*

El Terrorista – Hay Nanita / The Terrorist – Oh! Little Nan!
(Also, "There is a Little Nan") *(Bus)*

No Me Envidies – Imítame / Don't Envy Me – Imitate Me *(MFT)*

Solo Para la Muerte No Hay Envidia / Only for Death is There no Envy *(MFT)*

Viejo Pero Todavía.....Me Muevo / I'm Old, But I Can Still ... Move *(old car)*

Viejita Pero No Sea de Todos / I'm Old but not in All Things *(PT)*

Es Mi Trabajo No Es Herencia – "Gabrielita"
(This) Is My Work, Not My Office (or inheritance) – Little Gabriela *(PT)*

Principe Azul – Nubia / Blue Prince – Nubian (Slave?) *(SFT)*

PUEBLA

Gardénias / Gardenias *(painted on back of a flatbed nursery truck that was hauling manure!)*

No Somos Nada / We Are Nothing *(Bus)*
Zaragate / Little Rogue *(flatbed 18-T)*
Gitano / Gypsy *(MFT)*
Tigre Michel / Michel the Tiger *(MFT)*
Ya lo Hice ni Modo / No Matter, I Did It *(Bus)*

Para el Vino y las Mujeres Trabajamos los Choferes
We Truckers Work for Wine and Women *(MFT)*

PUERTO VALLARTA
Y Todo Para no Estudiar / All This for not Having Studied *(Bus)*

TBC Y TDG (Te Besé y Te Dejé) / I Kissed You and I Left You *(MFT)*

Sobre –– las Solas / Above All, Comfort! *(Assumes Solaz)*
(Or, if Solas, 'On Top of the Lonely Ladies' is a possible translation) *(MFT)*

Puros Jamones II / Pure Hams II – Pachuco *(LFT)*

QUARENTA Y CINCO
Rufian / Cad *(18-T)*

QUERÉTERO
Asi es La Vida – Albatros / That's Life – Albatross *(MFT)*
Palo Verde / Green Stick *(a tree) (green MFT)*

Oaxaca: "El ... Jefe" – Peligro / The Chief – Danger
This small farm truck was highly decorated, with skull and crossbones on its mudflaps.

SAN CRISTOBAL DE LAS CASAS
Así Es la Vida / That's Life *(a PT being used to drag dead bulls from the Corrida!)*

El Centaüro del Norte / The Centaur of the North *(LFT)*

Peligro – Alta Tensión / Danger – High Tension
(handpainted on the back window of a PT with camper)

Yaqui – Precaución es Vida / Yaqui – Be Cautious and Live *(DT)*

Llego el Rey de los Caminos / Here Comes the King of the Highways *(MFT)*

El Osito Panda / The Panda Bear
(particularly significant in Mexico since the birth of the baby in the Mexico City Zoo) (MFT)

SAN JUÁN DE LA PAZ
El Baron! / The Baron *(the oldest child) (MFT)*

SAN LUÍS POTOSÍ
Guëro / Blondie *(DT)*
Principe / Prince *(blue LFT)*
Big Foot II / Pie Grande II *(MFT)*
Gran Zocrates / Great Socrates *(DT)*
Eterno Caminante / Eternal Traveller *(LFT)*

* Malos * / Wicked Ones *(asterisks are pictures of eyes) (18-T)*

SAN MIGUEL DE ALLENDE
Mundadero / Worldly *(DT)*

Taxco: Pié Grande / Big Foot
The first time I saw this large farm truck in 1978, the radiator grill was intact
with the bumper dicho as shown. In December 1980, the grill was gone.
In April 1983, most of the foot and "PIE" had been scraped off in an accident.
This truck is native to Taxco, and is very hard used!

Taxco: Estóy Muy Linda "Visítame" / I am Very Beautiful, "Visit Me,"
This has to be considered an advertisement for the Hotel Posada de Los Castillo.
The hand lettering of the dicho, however, was enchanting enough to qualify for this book. (PT)

SANTA MARIA DEL RIO
Un Sueño de Todos – No Vale La Pena
A Dream of Everything – Not Worth the Trouble *(front bumper and windshield LFT)*

Se Ve Rica / (She) Appears Rich *(MFT)*
Aguila Solitario / Solitary Eagle *(Bus)*
El Maleficio / Evildoer *(LFT)*

TAPACHULA
Quemado / Burned! *(words surrounded by flames)*
(painted on both sides, front bumper, 18-T)

Duende / Spirit *(Hobgoblin) (18-T)*

El Guapo de Nebraska / The Handsome Nebraskan *(means 'ugly') (Bus)*
El Planetario 2000 / Astronomer 2000 *(Bus)*

TAXCO
Promesa Inutil / Useless Promise *(MFT)*
El Azúl Lado / The Blue Side *(SFT)*
El Bohe Mio / The Bohemian *(Bus)*
Blue Demon *(a well-known prizefighter) (MFT)*
Caminante / Traveller *(MFT)*
$ $ $ $ *(painted on back and sides of ore truck)*
Alma Grande / Great Soul *(SFT)*
El Mercenario / The Mercenary *(MFT)*
El Terrible / The Terrible One *(18-T)*
Caballero 2000 / The 2000th Gentleman *(MFT)*

Je, Je, Je, Ya LLegué / Hey, Hey, Hey, Here I Am *(LFT)*

Tierra Colorada / Red Land *(from Tierra Colorada City (MFT)*

El Colo de las Muebleros / The Ass of the Furnishers *(16-foot van truck)*

TAXCO
¡Una Vida de Tantas! – ¡Volveré! / A Life with So Much! – I'll Return *(Bus)*

SE SUBEN – Y SE BAJAN / They Rise – and They Fall
(words on the mudflaps under paintings of coastal highways)

Palomita / Little Dove *(small flatbed truck with a load of empty chicken crates)*

Así es La Vida / That's Life *(school bus full of children)*

Piel de Canela / Cinnamon Skin
(small truck painted cinnamon in color carrying a water storage tank)

El Tata Pitufo / Papa Pitufo
(Pitufo: a popular goblin in Mexico appearing as a TV show; a duplicate of USA smurfs) *(MFT)*

TEHUACÁN
El Mafioso / The Mafia Man *(MFT)*

TIERRA COLORADA
Leño / Firewood *(18-T carrying neatly-stacked lumber)*

Silver / Plata *(orange 18-T with silver ore)*
El Campeón / The Champion *(LFT)*
Guerrero Negro / Black Warrior *(18-T from the state of Guerrero)*

TOLUCA
El Bucanero / The Buccaneer *(MFT)*
El Padrino Primero / No. 1 Godfather *(SFT)*
Fujitivo / Fugitive *(DT)*
Highway Star—"Love Machine" *(LFT)*

*Taxco: * Linda Viajera * / Beautiful Voyager (SFT)*

Cíudad Juárez: Si Quiere Hacerse Millonário Compre Su Billete á Diario
If you Wish to be a Millionaire, Buy Your Ticket Daily.
Though not strictly speaking a dicho, this poem will serve as an example of the way in which
people are attracted to the many vehicles which sell tickets for the National lottery. (A walk-in van)

TUXPÁN
El Flaco / The Thin Man *(LFT)*

TUXTLA GUTIERREZ
Mi Pequeño / My Little One *(18-T)*
El Rey de Carretera / King of the Road *(MFT)*

VEINTE Y UNO
Rey Sin Palacio / King Without a Palace *(LFT)*

VILLA AHUMADA
A Tu Recuerdo – Y Como Es El – Muñeco
To the Memory of You – And How Is He? – Dollbaby *(LFT)*

YERMO
TRISTE––FELIZ / Sad––Happy *(left and right mudflaps, 18-T)*

ZACATECAS
El Samurai / The Samurai *(in bamboo script LFT)*
Latoso / Boring *(also annoying) (SFT)*
Mister Licores / Señor Liquors *(liquor truck)*
Sueño Imposible / Impossible Dream *(after a song of the same name) (LFT)*

ZITACUARO
Gitano Señorón / The Big Gypsy Man *(LFT)*

PANAMA

(Note: All are buses unless otherwise indicated)

PANAMÁ
El Son Cubano / The Cuban Sound
El Terrible / The Terrible
Sufre Ahora / Go Ahead and Suffer
Sigo Feliz / I'm Goin' on Happily
Soy Feliz / I'm Happy (with painting of singer)
Comparame / Compare Me (with other men)
Pura Sangre / Pure Blood(ed)
Puro Caldo / Pure Broth (Sauce)
Parece Mentira / It Appears You Lie
Mas Grande / (Its) Bigger
El Sonero Mayor / The Best Noisemaker

Mira lo que Encontré / Look What I Found

Mira lo que Tengo Detrás – Mira lo que Tengo Delante
Look What I Have in Back – Look What I Have in Front (referring to the dichos)

Juguete Caro – Inconsolable / Expensive Toy - (I'm) Inconsolable (back, front)

Sirenata en "B" / Siren in "B"
(a play on Sirena and Serenata with a painting of a siren on back door)

Sabroso – Autentica Calidad / Tasty – Authentic Quality
(front, back, with painting of Roy Rogers on backdoor)

Limpio pero Contento – Ejercito – Decimo Mandamiento
Clean (Liver) but Contented – Army – Tenth Commandment (front, side, back)

Pura Vida – El Auténtico / Pure Life – The Authentic (front, back)

El Jefe Soy Yo – Mandamas / I'm the Chief – The Big Shot! (front, back)

Panama: Lo Bueno, lo Malo, lo Feo / The Good, the Bad, (and) the Ugly.
After the American film of the same name. On the side of a bus.

*Peligro – Diesel * Alto Voltaje / Danger – Diesel * High Voltage*

Yo Soy la Ley – La Ley del Oeste / I Am the Law – The Law of the West *(front, side)*

Pacman – Trabajando Duro Por… / Pacman – Working Hard for…(What?) (side, back)

Especial Don Memo – El Sabor de lo Bueno
Mister Bill's Special – The Flavor of the Good *(both on side; otherwise undecorated)*

Hagas las Cosas en Mi Manera – No Es Tu Problema
Do Things My Way – It's Not Your Problem *(front, back)*

Y Como lo Hizo – Caligula / And How Did He Do It? – Caligula
(back, side; with painting of Caligula on the back door)

Rie Payaso – Sufren Ahora Payasos / Laugh, Clown – Clowns Suffer These Days
(back window and back; after Leoncavallo's "Ridi Pagliaccio;" with painting of sad clown)

El Desafio – Oficial / The Struggle – Official *(back, front)*

La Gloria de Carlos / The Glory (or Gloria his lady) of Carlos *(front)*

Calumnia / Slander *(painting of a sexy girl on back door)*

De Nada Vale Ser Bueno – Santos Jr.
It's Worth Nothing to be Good – Santos Jr. *(back)*

Yo Soy Feliz con Mi Toyota / I'm Happy with My Toyota *(back, "Corona")*

Atrévete / Be Bold! *(painting of Tom Selleck, back door)*

Puro Voltio – Apártate / Pure Voltage – (You'd better) Give Up *(back, front)*

Universidad de la Salsa / University for Salsa *(painting of torch singer, back door)*

Mas Vale las 30 que las 50 / It's Better to be 30 than 50 *(back)*

Panamá: Con lo Mio me Rio—Con lo Ajeno Peno / I Laugh with Mine—Others Give Me Pain (back)

PERU

CUSCO

Loco Cariñoso / Crazy (and) Loving (MFT)
Aventurero / Adventurer (MFT)
Danubio Azul / The Blue Danube (MFT)

Las Locas Illuciones Me Sacaron de Mi Pueblo
Crazy Dreams Drove Me from My City (from the song El Plebeyo, sung by Felipe Alba) (MFT)

Trome Apurimeño / Expert in Many Things (MFT)
TBC Luego TDG / I Kissed You then Left (SFT)

LIMA

El Chistos—Tony / The Crazy—Tony (Bus)
El Plebeyo / The Plebeian (MFT)
El Cheverón N° 4 / Super Duper No. 4 (MFT)
Los Comandos / The Commandos (MFT)
Bucanero / Buccaneer (MFT)
QUE RICO – QUE RICO / How Rich! (mudflaps, (MFT)
El Charrito / Little Cowboy (SFT)
El Verdugo II / The Scourge No. 2 (Bus)
El Machote / Super Macho (SFT)
El Todo Poderoso / All-Powerful

Niño Victor Poderoso / Child Victor the Powerful (MFT)

Pajita – Pulenta / Smooth – Tasty (Bus)

Chalan – San Martin de Pores
Cowboy (with special white costume) Saint Martin of Porres (MFT)

El Amigo de la Muerte / The Friend of Death (two MFTs)

Ho -- La?   Que... -- Tal?   Mas Amargo -- que Ayer...!
Hi! How Are you? More Distressed than Yesterday...! (back body, MFT from Huancayo)

LIMA
Adiós China Hereje – Gran Poder / Goodbye Sweet Heretic – Powerful *(MFT)*

Después de Mí…Qué Importa – Sr. Asunción de Cachuy
After Me…What Matters? – Jesus of the Assumption of Cachuy *(MFT)*

UNITED STATES OF AMERICA

ALBUQUERQUE, NEW MEXICO
Royal Knight / Caballero Reál *(hand lettered (PT)*

"Lonesome" / Soledoso *(hand lettered (18-T)*

ALGODONES, NEW MEXICO
Don Sanchez / Don (Mister?) Sanchez *(fancy lettering, tractor doors, 18-T)*

SANTA FE, NEW MEXICO
Speedy Gonzalez / Gonzalez Veloz *(front (18-T)*
Li'l Red Truck / Rojo Chico Camioncito *(PT)*
"Blue Angel" / Angel Azul *(with painted mountain scene; tailgate (PT)*
"Baby Hulk" *(light green PT of the same shade as the cartoon character)*

The Great Mountain Climber / El Montañero Famoso *(PT)*

ESPAÑOLA, NEW MEXICO
Bonnie & Clyde *(Fancy lettering, tractor doors, 18-T tank)*

* CHICO MALO *
JUAN ANTONIO
JUAN ANTONIO

DOBLE SENTIDOS

Izucar de Matamoros: Las Mujeres son como Las Carreteras Falsas Resbalosas y Traicioneras –
Que Tal Te Va Sin Mi – Albertito – Inocente – Triste Soñador – DAJESULUZ –
Women are like Highways: False, Slippery, and Treacherous – How are You Getting Along without Me?
– Little Albert – Innocent – Sad Dreamer – Jesus, Give Light (back);

INTRODUCTION

All dichos are at least double in meaning: the vehicle speaks both for itself and for the driver or owner. The other levels of meaning are largely amorous, or frankly sexual. One of the most universal of these, appearing in several forms, is:

Cambio Mi (Llanta) Vieja Por Tu Vieja
I'll Exchange My Old One (Tire) for Your Old One!

In *Soul of the Mexican Trucker*, Gloria Giffords illustrated a particularly egotistical Doble Sentido which I have seen in several countries with slight variations:

ME 109 CITO / I'm Feeling Renewed (Me Siento Nuevocito)
or My 109th One (Mi 109cito).

Most of the dichos in this Chapter are highly suggestive, though some milder ones are included elsewhere, especially in the chapter on Love and Lovers. I have suggested possible meanings, but the imagination is the best tool for supplying others.

Chico Malo – Juan Antonio.
Little Wicked Man – Juan Antonio (front, fancy "burro guard") (LFT)

INTRODUCCIÓN

Todos los dichos son por lo menode doble sentido: el vehículo habla por sí mismo, por el chofer o dueño. Los otros niveles del sentido son ampliamente amorosos o francamente sexual. Uno de los más universales de éstos, aparece en muchas formas, es:

Cambio Mi (Llanta) Vieja Por Tu Vieja

En *Soul of the Mexican Trucker,* Gloria giffords ilustró un Doble Sentido particularmente egoístico que ví en muchos países con algunas variaciones:

ME 109 CITO (Me Siento Nuevocito), o MI 109 CITO (Mi Cientonovecito).

Muchos de los dichos de este capítulo son sumamente sugerentes, aunque algunos más moderados aparecen en otras partes, especialmente en el capítulo sobre Amor y Amores. He un posible significado, pero la imaginación es la mejor herramienta para suplir otras.

ECUADOR

QUITO
Si Mas Tubiera Mas Te Diera / If You Had More I Would Give You More
(A milder version of the same dicho from Oaxaca) *(MFT)*

No Me Pase Cojudo / Don't Pass Me, Sucker
(This was substituted on the right side, back, in place of the usual No Pase — the left side having
Pite y Pase. The translation 'Sucker' or 'Fool' is a great deal milder than what was intended)
(MFT)

GUATEMALA

GUATEMALA
El Nuevo Sembradór / The New Seed-Spreader
(the farm! also, the name of a primary school text) *(MFT & Bus)*

Aquí Viene Tu Negro Santo / Here Comes Your Black Saint
(also one who is either very dear or slightly tarnished) *(black MFT)*

Me Dicen el Mil Amores / They Call Me 'The Thousand Lovers' *(MFT)*

Soy Feo Pero Sabroso / I'm Ugly but I'm Tasty (truck or owner?) *(MFT)*

Amante del Destino / Lover of Destiny (loves destiny or destined to be a lover?) *(PT)*

Te Vi Pués / So I Saw You (driver? lover? stop blowing your horn!) *(Bus)*

Llegó el Pelón / Baldy Has Arrived (also the name of the tow company: El Pelón) *(PT)*

Preciosa y ¿Que? / Precious and ...? (Also the bus company name) *(Bus)*

¡Picaré el Palomo! / The Cock-Pigeon Pecks! *(MFT)*

MEXICO

ACAPULCO
Mi Linda Crúz / My Beautiful Cruz (cross? cruise?) *(PT)*

Grito con Alma / I Cry Out with Spirit (alma?) *(Bus)*

CEBALLOS
Novillero / Herdsman (literally, one caring for heifers!) *(18-T)*

CIUDAD JUÁREZ
Corpus Christy / The Body of Christ...y! *(18-T)*

CHIHUAHUA
Las Curvas y Las Hoyos Me Están Consumido – Escorpión
The Curves and the Holes Have Emaciated Me! – Scorpion *(MFT)*

DOLORES HIDALGO
Dulce Sueños de Gloria / Sweet Dreams of Glory (Gloria?) *(SFT)*

IGUALA
El Rubensito / Little Ruben (also someone (del otro equipo), a 'gay' person) *(MFT)*

OAXACA
El Cantadór / The Singer (the enchanter?) *(MFT)*

El Palomo / The Cock-Pigeon (worthless fellow?) *(MFT)*

No Soy Dólar, Pero Subo / I'm Not (the) Dollar, but I Rise
(this same dicho is seen in several countries) *(MFT)*

Chata / Cutie (also, a snub-nosed man or truck, or a flat-bottomed boat; a bed pan)
(closed, walk-in PT)

Una en Mi Camino / There's One (Woman) on My Road! *(MFT)*

Cuídamela Virgencita / Take Care of It (Her) for me, Little Virgin (of Juquila)
(PT)

Hay Nanita! / Oh, Nanita! (Or, 'There's Nanita' or a cry of ecstasy?) *(SFT)*

Don Redondón / Mr. Five-by-Five (a play on words: Don appearing as 'mister,' and
as as part of Redondón, a large orbicular mass!) *(LFT with fat driver!)*

En Las Curbas Me Entretengo y en los Hoyos Me Detengo – Lolita
On the Curves I Entertain Myself, and in the Holes I am Detained – Lolita *(PT)*

Por Fin Cayó Mercedes / At Last, Mercedes Fell
(Mercedes was a printed sticker for a German car, but this *PT* was an old Dodge)

Si Lloras Quando Me Voy Que Sentiras Quando Me Llego – El Rey de los Caminos
If You Cry When I Leave, What Will You Feel When I Come – King of the Highways
(more egotism!) *(SFT)*

Guatemala: *Para Que Cortarlas Verdes Si Maduras Caen Solas – Brenda Maria*
Why Cut Green Ones When Mature Ones Fall by Themselves – Brenda Maria.
A moving bus photographed from a moving car; the sentiment could not be ignored!
The same dicho was also seen in Puebla, Mexico on a large farm truck.

Oaxaca: Si Más Tubiera, Más Te Metiera! / If I Had More, I would Give You More.
Tool Box (LFT)

PUEBLA
Vaquero de Noche / (Mid)Night Cowboy *(MFT)*

SAN CRISTOBAL DE LAS CASAS
Cámbio Mi Llanta Vieja Por Tu Vieja – Antonio
I('ll) Exchange My Old tire for Your Old One (Lady) – Antonio
(He had the guts to identify himself!) *(MFT)*

TAXCO
Guárdemelo, Virgencita / Keep it (the truck or what?) for Me, Little Virgin
(of Guadalupe) *(SFT)*

TEHUACÁN
Solicita Chamacon para Doblar la Lona
(We are) Looking for a Big Kid to Double the Burlap *(SFT)*

YAUTEPEC
Damemas Amor / Give Me More Love (loving) *(MFT)*

ZACATECAS
Corpus Christy / Body of Christy (from Corpus Cristi) *(18-T)*

Y No Le Hago en Barro / And I Won't Make It in Clay *(18-T)*

PANAMA

PANAMÁ
Caliente y Sabroso – Con Hambre / Hot and Tasty – (I am) Hungry
(back, front, Bus)

Caliente y Sabroso – Apolo / Hot and Tatsy – Apollo (front, side, Bus)

PERU

LIMA
Si Quiere Mas Polvo Sigame – José Manuél / If You Want More Dust, Follow
Me
(This translation is not what was intended: polvo is street slang for coitus.) *(dusty MFT)*

Oaxaca: Si Me Muebes Me Sacas Todo Lo Que Tengo
If You Move Me, You'll Take Everything I Have
Same large farm truck as previous photograph.

Oaxaca: Mi Nóvia ya no es Virginia – Principe / My Girlfriend is no longer Virginia
(or virgin?) – Prince. (LFT)

ANIMALITOS y CARICATURAS

Almalonga: EL CONEJO—DE LA SUERTE / Lucky—Rabbit.
These enchanting little rabbits in fancy dress and top hats were painted on well worn mudflaps
(SFT).

INTRODUCTION

The Indians of the Latin Americas believe that each person has an animal equivalent, a spirit called a 'Nahuál,' with which that person has a close and important relationship. As a result, animal figures appear frequently in weavings, in secular and religious folk art, and in paintings and dichos on vehicles. These dichos may be very humorous, or quite serious. Virtually every type of animal is represented, from the mouse to the elephant, from the hummingbird to the condor, and even turtles, snakes, and insects take their turns.

The dog, however, appears to be universally disdained: There are few references in dichos and few are flattering:

Mortifica Esta Perra / How this Bitch Embarrasses Me

or   Perro Callejero / Dog in the Street

Oaxaca: Cual es Tu Prisa / What's Your Hurry?
Decal on a medium farm truck with a number of dichos

INTRODUCCIÓN

Los Indígenas de América latina creen que cada persona tiene un animal equivalente, un espíritu llamado "Nahuál," con quien una persona tiene un relación unida e importante. Como resultado, figuras de animalitos aparecen frecuentamente en tejidos, en arte folklórico secular y religioso y en pinturas y dichos vehículares. Estos dichos pueden ser muy chistosos o totalmente serios. Virtualmente cada tipo de animal está representado, del ratoncito al elefante, del colibrí al cóndor, y hasta las tortugas, las víboras, y los insectos toman sus turnos.

El perro, sin embargo, aparece desdeñado universalmente. Hay pocas referencias en dichos, y pocas son lisonjeros:
Como Me Mortifica Esta Perra / o / Perro Callejero.

112

La Paz: Gran Gorila / Big Gorilla (MFT)

BOLIVIA

LA PAZ
Picaflor / Hummingbird (small Taxi)

ECUADOR

OTAVALO
El Diábolo / The Devil (Bus)
Demoño / Demon (Bus)

QUITO
A Caballo Vamos por el Monte / We Go to the Mountain on Horseback
(from a popular song) (MFT)

Reina del Cisne – Jesusito – Pite y Pase / No Pase
Queen Swan – Little Jesus – Honk and Pass / Don't Pass
(front, back, left back, right back, SFT)

Tiburón – Sarita Tarma / Shark! – Sarah Tarma (MFT)

La Mulita Baya N°1 / The Travelling Mule No. 1 (Vaya) (LFT)

Siempre Palomito Jr. / Always a Pigeon, Junior
(In Ecuador, Jr. is seen frequently on trucks and buses) (SFT)

Ya Llego Tu Palomo / Here Comes Your (Cock)-Pigeon (MFT)

Tu Palomo Parte … Ya! / Your 'Pigeon' is leaving … Now! (MFT)

Palomita Encantadera / Enchanting (Lady) Pigeon (MFT)

QUITO
No Se Acceptan *[Pavos]* / Turkeys (picture only) Not Allowed
(A rebus on the stair at the entrance to a Bus)

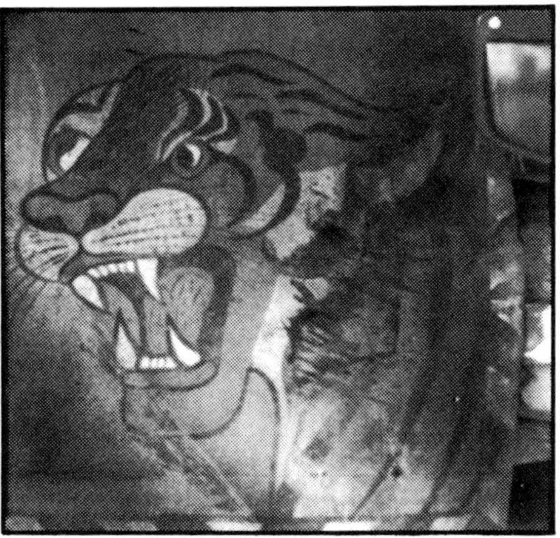

Lima: VICUÑTA—ERRANTE   Cusco: TIGRES
Paintings of Tigers and Travelling Vicuñas. One mudflap each from two 10-wheel produce trucks.

GUATEMALA

GUATEMALA
PATO – CITO / Little – Duck *(left & right mudflaps, MFT)*

Ave del Paraïso – Bird of Paradise *(Bus)*
El Puma / The Puma *(with a decal of a cobra) (Bus)*
El Pollito / The Little Chicken *(LFT)*

No dicho, but highly decorative gold and red eagles on each mudflap *(MFT)*

SALCAJÁ
Gatito / Little Cat *(Bus)*

MEXICO

ACAPULCO
El Bisonte / The Bison *(white (18-T)*
El Tigre / The Tiger *(white VW Bug Taxi)*
Mickey Mouse *(SFT)*

Lobo Rojo – Gran Jefe / Red Wolf – Big Chief *(DT)*

El Piolín / The Yellow Bird (a Hawser; Pio means pious or anxious desire, thus
The Pious One, or One with Litle Desire; also, Little Drunk, from the street slang Piolo, drunk.
Which was intended?) (MFT)

ACATLÁN
Aguila Roja / Red Eagle (red (PT)

AGUAS CALIENTES
Mula Azul / Blue Mule (blue (LFT)
"Porky" / Cochino (Tow Truck)
La Jila / The Gila Monster (SFT)

CHIHUAHUA
Escorpion II / Scorpion (or Scorpio) #2 (LFT)
Patito Feo / Ugly Duckling (SFT)
Potro Lobo / Pesky Wolf (MFT)

CHILPANCINGO
Búfalo / Buffalo (MFT)
Bisonte Blanco / White Bison (white MFT)
Albatrós / Albatross (MFT)
Solín / Solin (comic strip character) (MFT)
El León del Disierto / The Desert Lion (MFT)

CIUDAD JUÁREZ
La Paloma / The Dove (also, street slang for vagabond)
(spray-painted on back of 20-foot, white delivery Truck)

CUAUTLA
Caballo Blanco / White Horse (DT)

DOLORES HIDALGO
Caballo Loco 2° / Crazy Horse No. 2 (LFT)

CUENCAMÉ
Potro / Colt (SFT)

CUERNAVACA
Pato Salvaje / Savage Duck (18-T)
Búfalo Blanco / White Buffalo (MFT)
Sherif Lobo / Sheriff Lobo (seen in Lobo Canyon. The 'sh' sound does not exist in Spanish)
(LFT)

EL TREINTA
"Coyote" / Coyote (or 'half-breed') (Yoli Water Truck)

Oaxaca: Ave de Paso – San Francisco / Bird of Passage – "San Francisco"
(very fancy, with pictures of eyes at each end of front bumper) (LFT)

ETLA
Don Gato / Mr. Cat (LFT)

FRESNILLO
El Pajaro Prieto / The Dark Bird (MFT)

GOMEZ PALACIO
El Ala Crán / The Scorpion (18-T)
"Bugs Bunny" (LFT)

HUAJUAPAN DE LEÓN
Búfalo Rojo / Red Buffalo (red 18-T)
Mi Pequeño Panda / My Little Panda (SFT)

IGUALA
Fuera Pato / I (It) Would Rather Be (Go As) a Duck
(Whether from Ser or Ir, this imperfect subjunctive lends itself to a lot of interpretations) (Bus)

IXTAPAN DE LA SAL
El Pajarote / The Big Bird (Pajarota is Hoax) *(LFT)*

IZUCAR DE MATAMOROS
Pantera / Panther *(LFT)*

JIMÉNEZ
Ya Llego Viboras / Here I Am, Vipers (Gossips) *(LFT)*

MÉTEPEC
Gallo de Oro / Golden Rooster *(DT)*

OAXACA
PATO DE GOMA / Rubber Duck *(mudflaps, MFT)*
La Paloma / The Dove *(LFT)*
El Canario / The Canary *(yellow DT)*
TORO – MACHO / Bull – Macho *(red 18-T)*
Perro Callejero / Dog of the Street *(MFT)*
"Periquita" / Little Parakeet *(green PT)*
Peregrina / Traveller *(or Migratory) (PT)*
Conejo—"Bugs" / Rabbit—"Bugs" *(Bugs Bunny) (front & back, (MFT)*

"El Puma" – "Aracely" / The Puma – Aracely *(PT)*

Murmuren, Murmuren Vivoras / The Women (Snakes) are Gossiping (hissing)
(SFT & PT)

Oaxaca: Que Murmuren las Viboras – El Jefe / Why are the Vipers (Women) Hissing (Gossiping)?
– The Chief. Also, another version of Siga-Alto (MFT)

OAXACA
El Palomo / The Cock-Pigeon (worthless fellow) *(MFT)*

Tú Moras por una Mula ni Yo Que Perdi el Atajo – Paloma Herrante
You are Dying for a Mule and even I have Lost the Shortcut (Way) – Errant Pigeon
(SFT)

Escorpión 1ro / Number 1 Scorpion *(SFT)*

El Atravieso Pitufo & Los Pitufos / The Mischievous Smurf & The Smurfs
(with pictures) *(MFT and Bus, respectively)*

SAN LUÍS POTOSÍ
El Gallo / The Rooster *(18-T)*

SAN MIGUEL DE ALLENDE
La Gaviota / The Seagull *(Bus)*

SANTA MARIA DEL RIO
Canario/Irapuato / Canary/Irapuato
(Since Canario was above Irapuato, perhaps 'Canary over Irapuato' was intended!) *(SFT)*

TAMAZULAPAM
Mula * Azul / Blue Mule (with a picture at * of a mule bucking a rider) *(18-T)*

TAXCO
La Pichona – Padre Nuestro / The Pigeon – Our Father
(any relation to the Trinity?) *(SFT)*

*Taxco: An elaborate painting of an eagle on driver's door,
a very common pictorial theme in Mexico. (PT)*

Taxco: Painting of a Swordfish under the driver's door.
Large farm truck up from the Mexican west coast.

Moby Dick *(a 10,000 liter white tank truck carrying fuel)*

La Mula Azúl / The Blue Mule (MFT)
El Dragón Rojo / The Red Dragon (DT)
Oveja Perdida / Lost Sheep (LFT)

Como Me Mortifica Esta Perra / How this Dog (Bitch) Embarrasses Me! (MFT)

Fantasma / Phantom (or Scarecrow) (SFT)
El Super Ratón / The Super Rat (SFT)

El Grillito / The Little Cricket (VW Bus Taxi)

Lobo Rojo / Red Wolf (also decal on windsheild: "Racing Team") (MFT)

TOLUCA
El Condor / The Condor (18-T)
El Centauro – The Centaur (LFT)

TROPICO DE CANCER
Golondrina Viajera / Travelling Swallow (SFT)

TUXPAN
Dragon / Dragon (SFT)

VILLA AHUMADA
Lobo II / Wolf #2 (flatbed MFT)

YERMO
El Tiburón / The Shark (LFT)

ZACATECAS
El Gallo de Oro / The Golden Cock *(LFT)*
Gansito / Little Goose *(LFT)*

PANAMA

PANAMÁ
El Tigrillo / The Tiger *(black and orange Bus)*
El Escorpión / The Scorpion *(Bus)*
El Tiburón / The Shark *(small Taxi)*
El Pitufo / The Smurf *(SFT)*
Poseidon / Poseidon *(MFT)*

Noche de Perros / Night for Dogs *(with painting of dogs playing poker) (back door, Bus)*

Bicho Extraño / Strange Animal *(or insect) (PT made from a car with its roof off)*

Otra Vez La Bestia / The Beast Again *(very old (PT)*

(Las Estrellas) / Stars *(frequently painted on the back doors of buses.*
Examples: Charles Bronson; Tony Baretta; Peter Sellers; Linda Carter; Olivia Newton-John;
Barbra Streisand; John Wayne; Gene Autry; The Flintstones; Rocky Marciano.

Pony Exprez / Pony Express *(except it was a brick truck!)*

Papa Pitufo / Papa Smurf *(Bus with paintings)*
El Ranchero / The Rancher *(MFT)*

Caballo Viejo / Old Pony *(from a song) (very old PT)*

Sigo Plantando – El Peregrino IIdo / I Go On Planting – The Falcon No. 2 *(Bus)*

Giorgi / Georgie *(painting of a very 'sweet' dog) (Bus)*

PERU

CUSCO
El Gavilán Pollero / The Chicken Hawk *(also a man who persistently chases women)*
(MFT)

LIMA
Escorpión / Scorpion *(Bus)*
El Tiburón / The Shark *(Bus)*

MULTIPLES

Otavalo: Si Diós Quiere Volveré – Porque los Envidiosos Lloran por Mí – Comercial Caiza –
Comercial Pedrito – Super Ford 350 / If God Is Willing, I Shall Return –
Because the Envious Cry for Me? – Caiza and Little Peter Companies – Super Ford 350.
This MFT was parked in the marketplace, unattended.

INTRODUCTION

This chapter presents examples of two or more dichos on a single vehicle. It is of interest again to note the strong religious flavor which appears in all countries, especially in Guatemala. Usually, it is the large farm trucks which have the greatest number of dichos, but not always. Two trucks in Panama, a pickup and a large farm truck, had sixteen on each! The owner of the truck was enormously proud of his dichos, and enjoyed showing them off and allowing them to be photographed.

From Guatemala also came the most complex examples of what should be called "mudflap art": complex scenes painted onto the mudflaps of farm trucks. I have photographed some of the best examples of these scenes from the trucks which are used to haul sacks of sugar and flour to the Terminal Market in Guatemala City.

I was able to obtain only one dicho from El Salvador, but what a poetical one! It was inscribed on the mudflaps of a somewhat shop-worn pickup truck which had long been used for transporting produce.

Guatemala: La Patoja – Yo No Soy Abusadora – RISA ME DA—TUS DESPRECIOS
Little Scamp (back) – I am Not an A-bus-er (back bumper) – Your scorn—Makes Me Laugh (mudflaps

INTRODUCCIÓN

Este capítulo representa ejemplos de tres o más dichos en un sólo vehículo. Otra vez es interesante notar el sabor fuerte religioso que aparece en todos los países, especialmente en Guatemala. Usualmente son los camiones grandes de los ranchos que tienen la cantidad más grande de dichos, pero no siempre. Dos camiones en Panamá, un pickup y un camión grande de rancho, tenían dieciseis en cada camión. El dueño de estos camiones estaba enormamentc orgulloso de sus dichos y estuvo muy contento en mostrarmelos y en permitirme las fotografías que tomé!

De Guatemala también vinieron los más complejos ejemplos de "mudflap art": escenas complejas pintadas sobre los guardabarros (los mudflaps) de camiones de rancho. He tomada fotografías de los ejemplos mejores de estas escenas sobre camiones que se usan para cargar costales de azúcar y harina para el Mercado Ter-minál en la ciudad de Guatemala.

Pude obtener sólo un dicho de San Salvadór, pero que poético! Estaba inscrito sobre los guardabarros de un camión usado, estilo pickup, que ya tenía tiempo que se había usado para cargar verduras.

GUATEMALA

ANTÍGUA GUATEMALA
La Chica Vaciladora – Diós es Amor
The little Fickle One *(front)* – God is (True) Love *(tailgate)* *(Bus)*

GUATEMALA
Sufres al Verme – Diós Guide Mi Lupita
(You) Suffer to See Me (Back) – God, Care for my Lupita *(back)* *(Bus)*

No Te Olvides de Mi – Fé Amor y Caridád – SOMBRAS – NADA MÁS
Don't Forget Me *(front)* – Faith, Love and Charity *(back)* – Protected No More
(mudflaps) *(Bus)*

Ana—Eli – Risa Me Dá Tu Desprecio
Anna—Ellie *(front)* – Laughter Tells Me of Your Contempt *(back)* *(Bus)*

Nada Me Faltará – Jehovah es Mi Pastór / I Will Need Nothing *(back bumper)*
– (For) Jehovah is My Shepherd *(mudflaps)* *(MFT)*

SALCAJÁ
Gatito – Somos Diferentes / Little Cat *(front)* – We're (All Different) *(back)* *(Bus)*

SAN JUÁN SUCHITEPÉQUEZ
TUS DESPRECIOS—ME DAN RISAS – Cabeza pelona
Your Contempt Makes Me Smile *(mudflaps)* – Baldy *(front bumper)* *(MFT)*

MEXICO

ACAPULCO
El Arracadas—Amor Perdido – El Corsario / The Earrings (?)—Lost Love *(front)*
– The Corsair *(back)* *(Bus)*

CIUDAD JUÁREZ
Solo Para la Muerte No Hay Embidias – Se Doman Fieras al Domicilio –
Solo Diós Sabe Mi Destino / Only for Death There Is no Envy *(back body)*
– Wild Ones are (To Be) Housebroken *(back)* –
Only God Kows My Destiny *(front bumper)* *(MFT)*

CUAUTLA
Mi Consentido – Primero Diós y Volveré
My Spoiled One *(cab)* – God Willing I Shall Return *(front bumper)* *(MFT)*

CUERNAVACA

Paloma Viajera / Travelling Pigeon *(front bumper)*

| LAZ -- DE MI | The -- Of My |
| LLAVEZ -- ALMA | Keys -- Soul |

(mudflaps) (SFT)

OAXACA

San Judas Tadeo—Juquilita — Murmuren Vivoras – Visite Oaxaca – (León)
Saint Judas Tadeo — Little Virgin of Juquila *(front)* – Vipers (Women) are Hissing)
(Gossiping) *(back)* – Visit Oaxaca *(spare tire)* – (Lion paintings) *(mudflaps) (MFT)*

Hay Mira—Yo No Sé – La Chica del 87
Hey, Look—I don't Know *(back bumper)* – Miss Girlfriend of 1987 *(hood)*

MI *[corazón]* —— MISTER
ES TUYO —— BURRO
My Heart is Yours——Señor Burro *(front bumper by the license plate)*
('Corazon' is a heart drawn with Cupid's arrow through it) (PT)

Guatemala:
*Diós es Amor – Jesús La Lúz del Mundo – Una Vos de los Cielos Que Decia Tu Eres Mi Hijo Amado **
En Ti – Tomo Contentamiento / God is love – Jesus The Light of the World – (There Came) A Voice from
*the Heavens which Said 'You are my Beloved Son * (and) I Am Well Pleased' (left mudflap)*
Diós Te Ama – Jehova es Mi Pastór / God Loves You – Jehova is My Shepherd (right mudflap) (LFT)

Bién Has Hecho con Tu Siervo Oh Jehova, Conforme a Tu Palabra (Sal 119 V. 65)
Thou Has Dealt Well with Thy Servant, O Lord, According Unto Thy Word
Psalm 119, Verse 65, King James Version (left mudflap)
Jesú Cristo es el Mismo Ayér, y Hóy, y Para Los Siglos ([?] 13, v 8).
Jesus Christ the Same Yesterday, and Today, and Forever."
(Hebrews 13 Verse 8, King James version) (right mudflap)

Los Tres Consejos – Yó Te Recuerdo
Three Words of Advice *(front)* – I('ll) Remember You *(back) (SFT)*

Ladrón de Besos – Cuál es Tu Prisa? – Herminio Pérez Hernández – No Llevo
[Brujas] – No Te Hagas *[Toro]* – Servicio Particulár – Zimatlán, Oaxaca –
Si Más Tubiera Más Te Metiera! – Si Me Muebes Me Sacas Todo Lo Que Tengo
– Los Que en esta, Están Bailando, en el Otra Que Se Sientan
Stealer of Kisses *(front bumper)* – What's Your Hurry? *(hood)* – Herminio Perez
Hernandez – I Don't give Rides to Witches – Don't Make Bull! –
Private Service – Zimatlán, Oaxaca *(witch and bull are illustrations only, as are*
the eagle, shield and ducks) (front doors) – If I Had More, I Would Give You More
(left fuel tank) – If You Move Me, You'll Take Everything I Have *(right fuel tank)*
– Those Who (Are) In This Truck Are Dancing; Those in the Other, Are
Sitting *(back) (very well kept LFT)*

Soy El Mismo – Amira—Moíses – Ave Viajera – Cuídame Virgen de Juquila
I am the Same *(back bumper)* – Amira—Moses *(cab)* – Travellin' Bird *(truck or*
driver?) (hood) – Take Care of Me, Virgin of Juquila *(front bumper) (PT)*

Ave Sin Rumbo – Diós en Mi Camino – Hágase Señor Tu Voluntad
Bird without a Home *(spare tire cover)* – God (is) On My Highway *(cab)* –
Thy Will be Done, God *(front bumper) (LFT)*

No Te Illusiones Que Voy de Paso – El Gavilán Pollero – Innocente –
Pobre Amiga – Que Tal Te Vas Sin Mi
Have no Illusions that I'm Just Passing Through *(back bumper)* – The Chicken
Hawker *(Gavilán: sparrowhawk; Pollero: poulterer. Who knows what was intended)*

*Zuníl: Llorarás al no Verme – Tu Castigo es Verme – Pequeño Niño – Cierre Suave.
You Will Cry When You Don't See Me (tailgate) – Your Punishment is to See Me (lower tailgate) –
Little Child (hood) – Close Gently (driver's door with a decal of a horse) (blue (SFT)*

OAXACA

(front bumper) – Innocent *(front cab over windshield)* – Poor Friend *(girlfriend? truck?)*
(hood windscreen) – How Is It Going Without Me? *(hood) (LFT)*

Que Te Vaya Bonito - Coyote Montañero - "Kandukar" / May You Go Beautifully
(spare tire holder) - Coyote Mountaineer *(back body)* - Kandukar *(back bed) (MFT)*

Amor Sincero No Hay Como el de un Maizero – Para Los Invídios No Hay
Salvación / There's No More Sincere Love than Comes from a Corn Planter
(front) – There's No Salvation for the Envious *(back)*
(also a Racing Team decal on windshield) *(MFT)*

*Oaxaca: * El Muchacho Alegre * – Te Deseo con Todo Mi Amor – Kin-Kin. / The Happy Kid
(front bumper with flowers!) – I Desire You With All My Love (etched carefully on both windows
of the cab) – Kin-Kin (back body) (MFT) (see also page 51)*

*Oaxaca: El Crucero del Amor – Love Boat – Turismo Popular y Sociál / The Cruise of Love –
Love Boat – General and Group Tours. Greyhound Bus from a small company
which had chosen Love Boat as its theme! All the letters O are hearts.*

Ave Fenix – Juán Pablo II / The Phoenix – John Paul II (the Pope) *(MFT)*

Todos Los Que Me Ven Son Ojos – Diós Adelante y Yo en el Volante
All Who See Me are (Give me) Eyes (Back) – (Have Faith in) God, and
Forward (I go) Flying *(front) (PT)*

Adiós Amor – Diós y Suerte / Goodbye, Love *(back)* – God and Luck *(front)*
(also had a 'Texas Rangers' sticker on windshield) (truck)

Diós en Mi Camino – Bravo – Lorensito / (May) God Be (with me) On My Way
(front) – Angry *(back)* – Young Loren *(fringe, windshield) (FT)*

El Ahijovo de la Muerte – Me Recorderás – Jaimito – Aventurero
The Godchild of Death *(back body)* – You will Remember Me – Jamie – Adventurer
(SFT)

Me Recordarás – Si No Te Animas Pa Que Te Arrimas – Cuidado Ratas –
"Lupita" – Diós Es Todo Poderoso – You Shall Remember Me *(back bumper)*
– If You Don't Get Excited, Why Do You Come Near? *(spare tire holder)*
– Watch Out for (Female) Rats! *(fuel tank)* Little Guadalupe *(hood)* –
God is All Powerful *(front bumper) (LFT)*

Chava – Juguete Caro / Spinster *(hood)* – Expensive Toy *(body) (MFT)*

Diós Bendice el Trabajo del Hombre – Juguete Caro – Mi Chavito – "Emperador"
God Blesses Man's Work *(back bumper)* – Expensive Toy *(spare tire holder)* –
My Little Bachelor *(hood)* Emperor *(front bumper) (MFT)*

Oaxaca: Mi-Precio—UnosDolares $ $ - "Feli" - Niño—Vago
My Price—A Few Dollars (back) - Feli (hood) - Kid—Vagabond (front bumper) (SFT)

OAXACA

DiósArribaYoAbajoElMeGuíayYoTrabajo – Si Las Vacas Fueron Fieles
No Hubieron Tantas Buyes / God is Above and I'm Below; He Guides Me and
I Work – If Cows were Faithful, There would Be No Oxen (the first part with the
letters all run together, is a poem, according to the driver:
Diós Arriba, Yo Abajo
El Me Guía, y Yo Trabajo.
The second part is a double entendre with 'cows' for women and 'oxen' for fools) (MFT)

No Me Envidias—Imitame! – Bonetero – Galan / Don't Envy Me—Imitate Me!
(back bumper) – Bonnet Maker (cab) – Gallant (front bumper)(MFT)

Llamaré al Diós Altisimo al Diós que Me Faborece – Diós es Mi Escudo –
Cielito Lindo / I Shall Call to God the Highest, to God Who Favors Me
(back bumper) – God Is My Shield (front bumper) – Beautiful Heaven (sky) (cab) (SFT)

Me Duele Más Tus Adiós Que el Peór Castigo Que Me Imponga Diós –
Para el Vino y Las Mujeres Nacierón Los Choferes / Your Goodbyes Hurt Me
More than the Worst Punishment God Can Impose on Me (front) – Truck
Drivers Were Born for Wine and Women (back) (well-polished (MFT)

:Nomada: – Dueño de Nada – "Mundin" – Pájaro Azul
Nomad Lady (Back bumper) – Owner of Nothing (Spare tire holder) –
Worldly (Cab, over windshield) – Blue Bird (Front Bumper, M.F.T.)

!Casi,… un Angel..! – !Casi, Casi, Señorita!
Almost an Angel (Front) – Almost, Almost, Miss.
"Chevrolet" was also painted below. (P.T.)

Quién como Diós – DIÓS ES--* AMOR / Who (is there) Like God? (Back bumper)
– God is Love (On M-F's; a flower ("*") next to AMOR. (Fancy paintings of tropical
scenes, back windows camper shell) (P.T.)

OAXACA

Aquário – La Lúz De Tus Ójos Me Guía –
Deja Que Tus Ojos Me Vuelvan A Mirár
Aquarian (with palm trees) (Hood) – The Light of Your Eyes Guides Me (with musical
notes) (Front) – Allow Your Eyes to Look at Me Again (Back Body) (L.F.T.)

Yo [corazón] a Tehuantepec – AMOR DE ESTUDIANTE – ADIOS--ADIOS--
AMOR – "Alicia"
I Love Tehuantepec (The use of Hearts, as in 'I Love [heart] NY, is now seen a lot in Mexico,
and in other countries) Front bumper) – Love of a Student (Right Mud-flap) –·Goodbye--
Goodbye--Love (Left Mud-flap) – Alicia (Front Cab, over windshield) (M.F.T.)

Voy de Nuevo – La Colmena / Here I Am Again (Back) – The Bee Hive (Front)
Si No Tiene…Hoyo – No Es … Salvavidas! / If it Doesn't Have the Hole,
it isn't Life Savers' (Motorcycle Cart and driver!)

PUEBLA
$ $ $
No Hay Amor Sin Interes / There is No Love Without Interest
(a perfect double entendre! Note the $$$) (front bumper)

Oaxaca: Cóquis – Se Tanto Me Odias, Por Que No Te Mueres – Mátame Si Quieres Per No Me Olvides
Cóquis (a nickname from Socorro) (hood) – If You Hate Me So Much, Why Don't You Drop Dead?
(front bumper) – Kill Me if You Wish, but Don't Forget Me (back bumper) (PT)

Oaxaca: :La Paloma Es el Pájaro de la Paz: – SIMIMAMA YORO / the Dove is the Bird of Peace
(back) – Simimama Yoro (in bamboo script on spare tire).
The driver says this is a play on the phrase
Si Mi Mama Lloró: Yes, My Mother Cried; or, Yes, My Mother, I am Crying. He also says that the
dicho "La Paloma..." is a 'CRUDITY' of the worst sort!
Also paintings on mudflaps of sexy, well-dressed, sirens sitting on rocks by the sea. (MFT)

PUEBLA
No Llevo Brujas – Cada Quien Su Vida / I Don't Give Rides to Witches
(spare tire) – To Each His Own Life *(cab)* *(MFT)*

QUARENTA Y CINCO
Diós Te de Más de lo Que Tu Me Deseas a Mi – Amigo Organillero
May God Give You More than You Desire For Me *(back body)*
My Friend the Hurdy-Gurdy Man *(front)* *(SFT)*

SAN CRISTOBAL DE LAS CASAS
Yo Sufro Por Que Te Quiero – El Andarriego / I'm Suffering Because I Love You
(hood) The Traveller *(front bumper)* *(MFT)*

TAXCO
Que **F**elicidad Es **O**rer y **R**esar á **D**iós – Martha Lys--Dulce Ma.--Leonel Gerardo
What happiness it Is to Pray and to Worship God – Martha Lys--Sweet Maria--
Lionel Gerard. *(This dicho was uniquely written so as to include the metal letters 'F-O-R-D'
within its text.) (Hood, Pickup Truck)*

Virgencita de Guadalupe Bendice Mi Camino – Ud. de Azul—y Yo a Su Lado
– CHEVROLT / Little Virgin of Guadalupe, Bless My Way *(back)* –
(When) You (are) Blue—I('ll be) at Your Side *(Play on Azul and a su lado) (front bumper)*
(crudely painted frame) (MFT)

Malcriado – El Cordero de Diós / Ill-Mannered *(front bumper)* –
The Lamb of God *(hood) (MFT)*

Oaxaca: Diós Nunca Muere – ¿Donde Voy?....¡A La Féria! – El Famoso – Oaxaqueño Ausente –
Martha / God Never Dies *(front bumper)* – Where Am I Going?...To the Fair! *(back body)* –
The Famous *(frame under)* – Absent Oaxacanian *(spare tire)* – Martha *(front) (small carnival truck)*

TAXCO

Perro / Médico De Las Locas / Dog *(hood)* – Doctor to the Crazy Ladies
(front bumper) (MFT)

Rey de Reyes – Chely—Lety—Paco—Magda—Susy / King of Kings *(front bumper)*
– Names *(hood) (LFT)*

Pasa Me – Una Hermana / Pass Me *(clear instruction, back bumper)* – A Sister
(new instruction! front bumper) (farm truck)

Another version of this is Pasa Me & Tu Hermana / Pass Me – Your Sister (which, in the case of one
taxi in Taxco, led to a police infracción, with consequent removal of the dicho from the vehicle!)

La Pichona – Padre Nuestro / The Pigeon *(hood)* – Our Father *(front) (SFT)*

TUXTLA GUTIERREZ

Bucanero / Buccaneer *(back)*
Selos Dije – I Told You So! *(front) (MFT)*

ZUNÍL

Si Diós Conmigo – Quién Contra Mi? – Mitsubishi
If God is With Me, Who Is Against Me?
'Mitsubishi' was a fancy windshield fringe. Mickey Mouse pictures on Mud-flaps, with Niño – ???
(second word not decipherable, could be Vago, 'Vagabond Kid') (A Large Farm Truck)

*Lima: " "Odiame No Venganza" " – *Al Verme Sufres [corazón]* – "El Viajero" – No Se Gana*
pero Se Goza – Me Voy Pero... ...Volveré Corazón – (Condores)
Hate Me, but No Vengeance – You Suffer when You See Me, Love (My Heart) – The Traveller –
You Never Win Without Enjoying Yourself – I'm Going but...I'll Be Back!
Paintings of Condors (both mudflaps) (SFT)

Panamá: Ay Como No – Voy 'Palante – Mi Dally – Pura Vida (sides) –
Como Te Quedó el Ojo – OFI – To Ta Hablao (top front) –
No Me Tratas Así—Necio – Cuál Es Tu Apuro! – Ay Como No – Guarde Su Distancia (back) –
Why Not? – I'm Moving Ahead – My Dolly – Pure Life –
How's Your (black) Eye? – Official – All Has Been Said –
Don't Treat Me That Way, Stupid! – What's Your Hurry – Why Not? – Keep Your Distance

PANAMA

PANAMÁ

Buenos Momentos – Tu lo Has Dicho – Decisión / Good Times (back window) –
You Said It! (front) — Decision (back bumper)
(painting of Mayflower-type boat with three masts and crossed flags of Panama, back door) (Bus)

Milagrosa – Super Cat 40 – Mundo Latino / Miracle Worker (painting of Virgin)
(back door) – Super Gato 40 (side) – Latin World (back) (Bus)

Libertad – Paz y Amor – Panama Libre – Cayendo Vayan – Ejemplo de Paz
Liberty (front) – Peace and Love (side) – Free Panama (side) – They are Falling
(back) – Example of Peace (back) (Bus)

Amigo de Qué – Luchar Es Vivir –
No Quiero Manzanillo *(Front)*
Friend of Whom? *(see back)* – To Struggle is to Live –
I Don't Like Threesomes
Amigo de Qué – Diós Siempre en Mi Camino *(front)*;
Amigo No Hay – y..... Ahora Qué *(left, rear M-F)* – Deja Que Digan – Vamos a Dejarlo Ahí
(right, rear M-F); Rumbo al Darién – Lo Mio Es Mio – Mano Limpia *(right, front M-F)*
– Monte Adentro *(left, front M-F)* – Diesel *(fuel tank)* – De Un Amigo Mio *(right side
mirror)* – Mano Limpia – Llegaste Tarde *(right side mirror)*

*Panamá: Quando Estabas....en la Buena no Te Quejabas . – Ahora Sufre – Callao – Mano Limpia –
Quien Dijo Miedo – Vamos a Dejarlo Ahí – Amigo No Hay (back)
When You Had it Good...You Didn't Complain – Now, You Suffer –
In Silence (callado) – Clean Hand(s; Living) – Who Said (I'm) Afraid? – We're Going to Leave it There
(allí) – There is No Friend (see front). First Sergeant Rito Salgado Quintana of the Marina
(see photograph) where this, and the next truck were found, is very proud of his vehicles and of
the dichos he painted on them!*

PANAMÁ
Who's Friend? – God (Is) Always (With Me) On My Way
There Is No Friend – and.....Now What? – Let 'Em Gabble – We'll Leave it
There – Bound for Darien – (What's Mine Is Mine – Clean Hand – Climb In! –
Diesel (very fancy) – From a Friend of Mine – Clean Life – You Came Late! (On
this M.F.T. are example of much of the folk-art which this book is about!)

PERU

LIMA
Amor de Estudiante – Bandido – De Frontera a Frontera
Student's Love (front bumper) – Bandit (front) – From Frontier to Frontier (side) (LFT)

Algún Dia la Pagarás – Lucianino – (TIGRES) / Someday You Will Pay for It
(grill) – Man from Lucanos (front) – Painting of Tigers (mudflaps) (MFT)

El Caminante—Mi Freddy – Ese No Es Nada – Egualito Es – (CONDORES)
The Traveller—My Freddy – This is Nothing! – It's Equal – Painting of Condors
(mudflaps) (SFT)

El Fugitivo y Sus Alludas – Cruz de Guadalupe – Juany—El Fugitivo Beto –
Si Tu lo Haz Decidido Así Qué le Vamos a Hacer
The Fugitive and his Allies (windshield) – Cross of Guadalupe (hood) – Johnny—
The Fugitive 'Beto' (nickname) (back body) – If That's What You Have Decided,
What Are We Going to Do About it? (back bumper) (Bus)

Guíame Sr. de los Milagros – Los * Hombres * por * el * Amor * y las * Mu-
jeres * por Interes – Virgen de la Asunción
Guide Me, Christ of Miracles (Hood) – Men for Love, Women for Interest! (Grill)
– Virgin Mary of the Assumption (Top, Front; M.F.T.)

*Lima: Solo Te Queda Mirarme – Mi Nobleza Perdona Tu Ignorancia – Diós Es Amor
– Fé Al Sr. DeMuruhuay
You Only Stay (with me) Out of Admiration (front bumper) – My Nobility Pardons Your Ignorance
(back bumper) – God Is Love (windshield) – Faith in Christ of Muruhuay (front body) (Bus)*

LIMA
El Amor de Medianoche – Se Recibe Carga – Taxi Libre
Midnight Lover – We Accept Cargo – Free Taxi *(An old Pickup truck in the market)*

EL SALVADOR

SAN SALVADOR
Voy Caminando   Irving
Camino Solo Por Andár
Te Miro y Parece Que Está Ida

I am Travelling; I Travel only to be Travelling, I look for You and (but)
It Appears You Have Gone *(left mudflap)*

Lloro Por Llorár y Nádie
Llora Solo Por Llorár
El Andarriego

I am Crying for (I must be) Crying, and (but) No one Cries Solely for the
Sake of Crying — The Traveller *(right mudflap) (PT)*

Juan Aldama: Esto Es Amor / This is Love
This decal was one of many on a fancy SFT (see also page 129)

Oaxaca: "Baby Face" – "Carita de Niño"
One above the other on an LFT

INTRODUCTION

This Chapter has been reserved for dichos which clearly fall into more than one category and are not 'multiples.' One of these *retazos* is political (page 143). What made it particularly interesting was not only its uniqueness, but also that someone, presumably from another party, had mutilated it. We are not used to such mutilation of bumper stickers in the United States of America, but then we tend not to express ourselves as freely and openly as the Latins.

Another small but interesting element in this Chapter is the trio of toys: an airplane, a truck, and a pair of buses, each with its own dichos. Thus, one folk art is preserved in another.

Lima: Un Fracaso Más Que Importa – VICUÑITA—ERRANTE
One More Failure, Who Cares? (back, body) = Travelling Vicuña
(with paintings of vicuñas and mountain scenery on the mudflaps) (MFT)

INTRODUCCIÓN

Est Capítulo está reservado para dichos que claramente caen en más de una categoría, y que no son "multiplics." Uno de estos retazos es político (pagina 143). Lo que lo hizo particularmente interesante no fué sólo su raridad, pero también que alguien, por presunción de otro partido, lo había mutilado. No estamos acostumbrados a la mutilación de bumper stickers en los Estados Unidos de América, pero también no estamos acostumbrados a expresarnos tan libremente como los latinos!

Otro elemento pequeño pero interesante en este capítulo es una triada de juguetes: un avión, un camión, y un par de autobuses, cada uno con sus propios dichos. Entonces, un arte folkfórico está preservado entre otro!

BOLIVIA

LA PAZ
Tal-Tal / So-So (Bus)
Oh Linda La Paz / Oh, Beautiful La Paz (Bus)

ECUADOR

OTAVALO
Tiro Fijo / I Shoot Straight (Bus)
Así Es Mi Vida / That's My Life (SFT)
Una Chulla Vida / A Jackanape's Life (MFT)
Qué Béstia Es Mani / What a Beast is Mani (MFT)

Jesús de Gran Podér – Servicio de Lujo
Jesus of Great Power – Luxury Service (SFT)

QUITO
Hasta la Vuelta / So Long! (SFT)
Quito Yo Te Amo / Quito I Love You (Bus)
I Love Quito / Yo Amo a Quito (Bus)
Sin Comentarias / Without Comment (Gossip) (Bus)
Avante / Energetic (MFT)

*Quito: Mucha Nota – No Me Mires Mas – Nº 1 – 5 m Promiso – Pite y Pase – No Pase
Sees a Lot – Don't Admire Me More (left) (Bus) – Without Commitment (**Sin Co**mpromiso) –
Honk & Pass – Don't Pass. Both ceramic buses were for sale in the store, **La Bodega***

Oaxaca: El Salário del Miedo / The Wages of Fear
The Spanish version of the American movie (LFT)

QUITO

Tumbo, Tumbo / Outcast! (rejected; passion flower) *(Bus)*

Siempre Adelante—Reina del Camino—Carlitos Jr.
Always Forward—Queen of the Highway—Carlos Jr. *(MFT)*

Pero Sigo Siendo El Rey / But I Go On Being the King *(SFT)*

A Vezes Si a Vezes No / Sometimes Yes, Sometimes No *(MFT)*

Es Un Ford – Es Un Ford – San Vincente
It's a Ford – Saint Vincent *(SFT)*

GUATEMALA

ANTÍGUA GUATEMALA

Sonríele al Viejo Como Me Sonries a Mi
Smile at the Old Man As You Smile at Me *(SFT)*

Vive y Deja Vivir / Live and Let Live *(Bus)*
Páz y Bién / Peace and Good (will) *(Bus)*

Quando Una Vida está en Peligro Nadie Lleva la Via
When a Single Life is in Danger, No one Makes Headway *(Bus)*

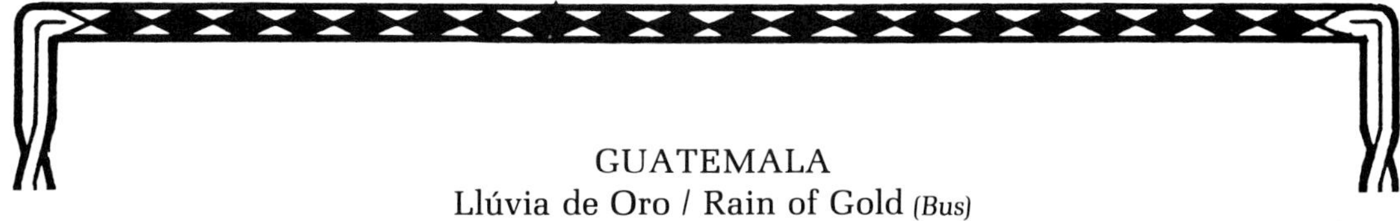

Llúvia de Oro / Rain of Gold *(Bus)*
Pero No Se Enoje / But Don't Get Mad *(Bus)*
Le Pese a Quien Le Pese / He Who Regrets, Regrets *(MicroBus)*

Quito: Henrry Joffre – Es Un Ford – Es Un Ford / Henry Joffre / It's a Ford – It's A Ford.
This is a typical Ford truck in Ecuador: it displays the pride of its owner. Another type of truck
is seen below, from the collection of Pete Cecere:
Solo Queda los Recuerdos / Only Memories Remain

MEXICO

ACAPULCO
Alma De Niña / Soul of a Little Girl (MFT)

AGUAS CALIENTES
Los Pastores / The Shepherds (SFT)
Corcel III / Steed III (MFT)

BERMEJILLO
Noche Negra / Black Night (beautiful, too!) (18-T)
El Día / The Day (18-T)

CAMARGO
El Fín de las Discórdias / The End of the Arguments (LFT)

CEBALLOS
El Solar / The (truck? of) Noble Lineage (22-T)

Alazan Tostado / Toast-Brown Sorrel Horse (red brown LFT)

Juán Aldama: Alma Alejandra / Alexandra's Soul
There were also many decals: one, of the famous panda bears saying Esto Es Amor;
others, of all sorts of animals. A dicho on the front bumper was almost faded away, and illegible.
(SFT) (see also page 138)

CHIHUAHUA
El Mil Usos / (Truck of) Thousand Uses *(MFT)*
El Pequeño / The Little One *(SFT)*

El Mojoso / The Marinater (from Remojo, Mojo is used in Mexico for sauce or marinade,
as in Mojo de Ajo: garlic marinade) *(MFT)*

Volveré / I Shall Return *(MFT)*
Adiós Chavo / Bye-bye Kid *(LFT)*

CIUDAD JUÁREZ
El Recorrido / The Route *(PT)*
La Colorina / The Showy One (red *(SFT)*

CUAUTLA
Pocho / Rotten *(LFT)*

Pura Bencidrina / Pure Benzedrine *(LFT)*

CUERNAVACA
La Popa / The Stern (nautical) *(SFT)*

CUILAPAN
No Para Ser Servido – Síno Para Servír
Not to Be Served, but to Serve *(VW Rabbit)*

DELÍCIAS
Pipiolo / Beginner (the o and the l of pipiolo were run together) *(MFT)*

ÉTLA
Cebollón / The Big Onion *(18-T carrying onions)*

Gerente / Director *(LFT)*

Ciudad Juárez: Chago Nieto Amigo – PRI – 1983-1986
Santiago Nieto – Friend 1983-1986 – The Institutional Revolutionary Party

GUZMAN
El Buque / The Freighter *(SFT)*

IXTAPAN DE LA SAL
el KONTIKI sol / the KONTIKI sun *(18-T carrying ore)*

IZUCAR DE MATAMOROS
CB5 Patito CuaCua – A Diós Sea La Gloria
Little Duck Quack on CB Channel 5 – To God Be the Glory
(Channel 5 is equivalent to our Channel 19) (MFT with CB)

As de Oros / Ace of Diamonds *(several LFTs)*

Sigusta—Súbete / If You Wish—Climb On *(SFT used for transporting people)*

Mi Précio—Unos Cuentos / My Price—Some Stories *(back) (SFT)*

JIMENEZ
Ajita / Little Red *(as chili) (red 18-T)*
El Amarillo / The Yellow One *(brown! MFT)*
El Estudiante / The Student *(18-T)*

MÉTEPEC
El Chubasco – Lasarito / The Stormy One – Little Lazarus *(SFT)*

MÉXICO DF
Toco No / I Touch Not…*(MFT)*
No Que No Hablados / Nothing but Gossip *(MFT)*

Mi Negro *(and a decal of U.S. flag)* / My Black *(or Darling what?) (Bus)*

MORÉLIA
El Arracadas / The Pendant Earrings *(seen three times. It is interesting that it is El
each time, though arracada is feminine; man with earrings?) (Bus)*

MOROLEÓN
"Seven Leven" *(LFT)*

Calzonuda / The Emperor's Clothes *(from calzón and nuda) (panel truck)*

OAXACA
Payasito – Quo Vadis? / Little Clown – Where do you Go *(Bus)*

Pluma Hidalgo / A Courteous Pen *(MFT)*
El 7 Mares / The Seven Seas *(LFT)*
¡ Fantomas ! / Phantoms ! *(spare tire) (MFT)*
Piedras Negras / Black Rocks *(Tank Truck)*
Palabras Tristes / Sad Words *(PT)*

OAXACA
Dos Angelitos / Two Little Angels *(SFT)*
1° de Julio / The First of July *(Bus)*
El Tío / The Uncle *(Bus)*
Plebeyo / Plebeian *(MFT)*
No Vale La Pena / Not Worth the Trouble *(Bus)*
Motivos! / Motives! *(Bus and DT)*
Mestizo / Half-breed *(LFT)*

Vendrán Sin Rumbo – Señor Hagace Tu Vuluntad
They'll Come without Pomp – God, Thy Will Be Done *(SFT)*

Cazador de Espiritus – Eso / Ghost Hunter *(front)* – That's It! *(back)* *(MFT)*

Cada Quien Su Vida / To Each His Own Life *(SFT)*

El Banbino—"Pelusa" / The Baby—"Fuzzy" *(SFT)*

PÁTZCUARO
Barbas / Beards *(MFT)*

PUEBLA
Diós y Hombre – Campeón / God and Man – Champion *(MFT)*

Panamá: # Zapatero Paga Doble # / No Jueges con Mi Libertad
Cobbler Pays Double (with dominos) / Don't Play With My Liberty.
The first is the sobrenombre (nickname) of my taxidriver, Adriano Morelos;
The second shows Adriano with an old, defiant bus!

PUERTO VALLARTA
Caricas Baratas / Cheap (Kidney) Beans (Bus)

RIO GRANDE
Bandolero / Highwayman (18-T)
Bonanza / Prosperity (MFT)

SAN CRISTOBAL DE LAS CASAS
Paintings of a Cove, the Sea, a Boat, a Coastal Highway (mudflaps) (MFT)

El Granaja de GRO / The Farm of GRO (Guerrero?) (MFT)

SAN GABRIÉL CHILÁC
Caprichoso / Capricious (playful) (MFT)
Vuelve á la Vida / Come Back to Live (SFT)

SAN LUÍS POTOSÍ
Tras Una Ilución / It's an Illusion (LFT)
Chapao / Plated (from chapado?) (MFT)

SAN MIGUÉL DE ALLENDE
Me Critican Por… / They Criticize Me for …(PT)

Panamá:
Necesito Tu Amor – Palo….Con Ella – Diós Es Mi Guía – El Santeñito Guapo – Peligro Alto Voltaje.
I need your Love – Stick (a double meaning) with Her – God Is My Guide
The Handsome Boy from Santeños
Danger High Voltage! (On a cold drink cart?) The best decorated push cart I have seen!

Panamá: Mas Na – La Nave del Olvido / More Than Anything – Ship of Forgetfulness.
First is from Mas Que Nada and refers to the festival of Penonome, Panamá; the second after a book
Both are from Panamá interior buses.

SAUCILLO
Paleta / Palette
(A personal favorite. Many dichos look like the many colors on a palette.) *(18-T)*

TAXCO
Jazz / Jazz *(scratched crudely in the back bumper paint of a SFT)*

Forastero / Forrester *(SFT with a load of wood)*

TECAMACHULCO
Escuadra Torres – Torres' Squad *(MFT)*

TECOMAVACA
Barrio Pobre / Poor District *(MFT)*
Zayonara / Sayonara (So Long) *(SFT)*

Peace * and * Love *(Peace symbols were painted where the asterisks are) (SFT)*

TEHUACÁN
Vero / True! *(MFT)*

TOLUCA
Dueño de Nada – Maria de Jesús / Chief of Nothing – Maria of Jesus *(LFT)*

VEINTE Y UNO
Pura Ilusión / Pure Illusion *(LFT)*

XALITLA
El Concentido / The Spoiled One *(this macho VW Bug was!)*

YANHUITLÁN
El Moro de Cumpas / Wine among Companions
(Cumpa is a South American word; the intent is not clear) *(LFT)*

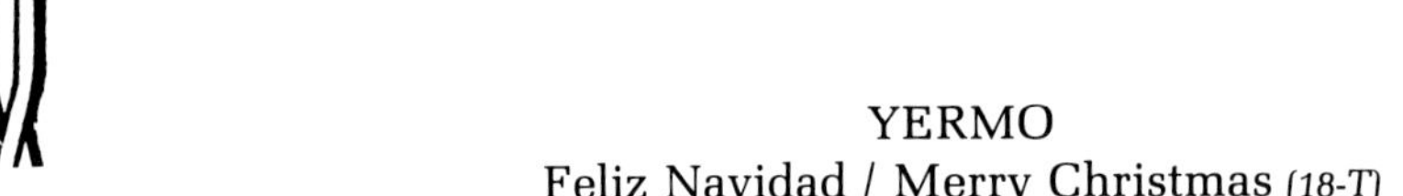

YERMO
Feliz Navidad / Merry Christmas *(18-T)*

ZACATECAS
Cascabelito / Little Rattlesnake *(medium TT)*
Pequeña Ilusión / Little Illusion *(PT)*
Rio Colorado / Red River *(DT)*
Fuereño II / Hick No. 2 *(MFT)*

ZITACUARO
El Silencio II / The Silence No. 2 *(MFT)*

PANAMA

PANAMÁ
Límpio Pero Contento – X Mandamiento
Clean but Content – 10th Commandment *(Bus)*

Juntos Todo Es Posible / Together Everything is Possible *(Bus)*

Algo Diferente – Pura Vida Pana / Something Different – Pure Pana(ma) Life
(Bus)

Voy a Balaso / I'm in a Terrific Hurry *(Bus)*

Parece Mentira / It Appears You Lie *(Bus)*
No Es Laca / That's No Lie! *(Bus)*
¡¡Hola Amigos!! / Hi, Friends !! *(SFT)*
Hola Pma / Hello There, Panamá *(Bus)*
Ahora Si! / Now, Yes! *(pushcart)*
Qué Humanidad / What Humanity! *(taxi)*
Nueva Vida / New Life *(Bus)*
Pura Vida / Pure Life *(Bus)*
Navidad Alegre / Merry Christmas *(Bus)*

Lima: + Angelito +
Little Angel (being painted on the hood by one of the professionals in the Barrio de los Gitanos)

PANAMÁ
Quién Creyera / Who Would Believe It? *(Bus)*
Charco Azul / Blue Puddle (lake) *(Bus)*

Voy Palante – Tratame Bién – Expreso Rodríguez
Going Ahead *(para adelante)* – Treat Me Well – Rodriguez Express
(back bumper) (front) (side) (Bus)

Aquí Siempre – Adiós y Grácias / Always Here! *(front)* / Goodbye and Thanks!
(back) (Bus) Front-back pairs like this are common

De Todas Maneras Risa – Frente a Mi / In Any Case, Smile – Stand By Me
(Bus)

Ahora Si – Venceremos / Yes, Now – We Shall Conquer
(painting of a Viking, back door) (Bus)

Mejor Tiempo Vendré – El Capricho de un Progresista
Better Times Are Coming *(front)* – The Caprice of a Progressive *(back) (Bus)*

Ritmo de la Vida / Rhythm of Life *(painting, Panamanian voodoo drummer, back door) (Bus)*

PERU

CUSCO
Trabajo No Me Envídias *(SFT)*
Trabaja y No Envídias – Diós Es Mi Guía *(Bus)*
Work and Don't Be Envious! – God Is My Guide
(Many versions of these combinations were seen)

Los Angeles Azules – The Blue Angels *(Bus)*
Provincianito / (I'm) From the Provinces *(SFT)*

El Fruto de Tus Envidias / The Fruit of Your Envy *(Bus)*

La Envidia Es Tu Venganza / Jealousy Is Your Revenge *(SFT)*

Siempre Adelante Con Fe y Valor / Always Ahead with Faith and Courage
(oil truck)

Liwi / Sling *(Quechua word) (MFT)*

LIMA
Ponte Mosca / Step on the Gas! *(MFT)*
Rayo de Luz / Ray of Light *(MFT)*
Perverso—10 / Perverse No. 10 *(MFT)*
Cielito Lindo / Beautiful Sky *(MFT)*
Luchador / Lighter! *(MFT)*
Raudál / Lots *(MFT)*
La Ponderosa / The Pine *(MFT)*

LIMA

Las Intocables / The Untouchables (MFT)

Quita Qué Te Tumbo / Stop or I'll Tumble You (two (MFT)

La Fé Que Lucha – San Martin de Porres / Faith Battles / Saint Martin of Porres
(MFT)

[corazón] Flecha Velóz [corazón] / Speedy Arrow
(paintings of hearts with arrows) (bright red (SFT)

Alma—Coraón—y Vida / Spirit—Love—and Life (MFT)

Niño Salvador Ayudame – "HOLA!" --- "HOLA!"
"CHAO!" --- "CHAO!"
Christ (Child), Savior, Help Me! – Hello, Hello, Goodbye, Goodbye
(Ciao in Italian means hello; in the Americas, goodbye) (MFT)

Dates	City	Signs	Vehicles
Jan 20 thru Feb 18	Oaxaca	Acuário - Aquarius	PT
Feb 19 thru March 20	Bermejillo	Piscis - Pisces	LFT
March 21 thru April 19	Taxco	Ariense - Aries	18-T
April 20 thru May 20	Iguala	Tauro - Taurus	MFT
May 21 thru June 21	Guatemala	Gemelos - Gemini	Bus
June 22 thru July 22	Toluca	Cancer - Cancer	18-T
July 23 thru August 22	Oaxaca	Leo - Leo	LFT
August 23 thru Sept 22	Oaxaca	Virgo - Virgo	MFT
Sept 23 thru Oct 23	Jimenez	Libra - Libra	MFT
Oct 24 thru Nov 21	Chihuahua	Scorpio - Scorpio	LFT
Nov 22 thru Dec 21	Oaxaca	Sagitario - Saggitarius	LFT
Dec 22 thru Jan 19	Panama	Capricornio - Capricorn	Bus

Oaxaca: "Sagitario / Saggitarius (18-T)

QUIEN SABE

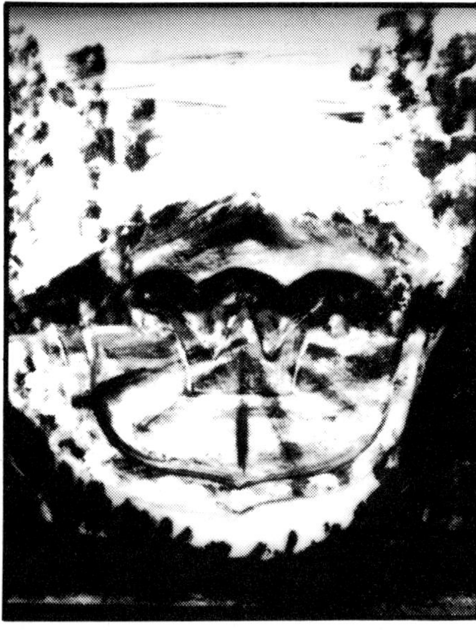

Oaxaca: Mudflap paintings of mountains capped with snow, something which is only seen on the great volcanoes like Orizaba, which these mountains most closely resemble. (MFT)

INTRODUCTION

The dicho is a saying, a part of an oral tradition and, thus, not readily identifiable in a dictionary. The letters of such dichos are often written phonetically without a letter which is silent, like H, or with letters exchanged: such as

B for V / C for Q / C for K / F for V / G for H / J for G / LL for Y / S for C and vice versa!

Given the frequency of misspellings, the grammatical 'liberties,' and the fact that the author of this book does not have an extensive familiarity with the street slang of all the countries, the task of translation has often been difficult.

I was unable to arrive at a solid translation for the dichos in this Chapter. What was intended by the vehicular painter? These persistently mysterious dichos have been included for three reasons: first, because some passionate soul went to the trouble to paint them onto a vehicle; next, because they are tantalizing; and, finally, because some reader might know the meaning or have some good suggestions as to what the translation might be.

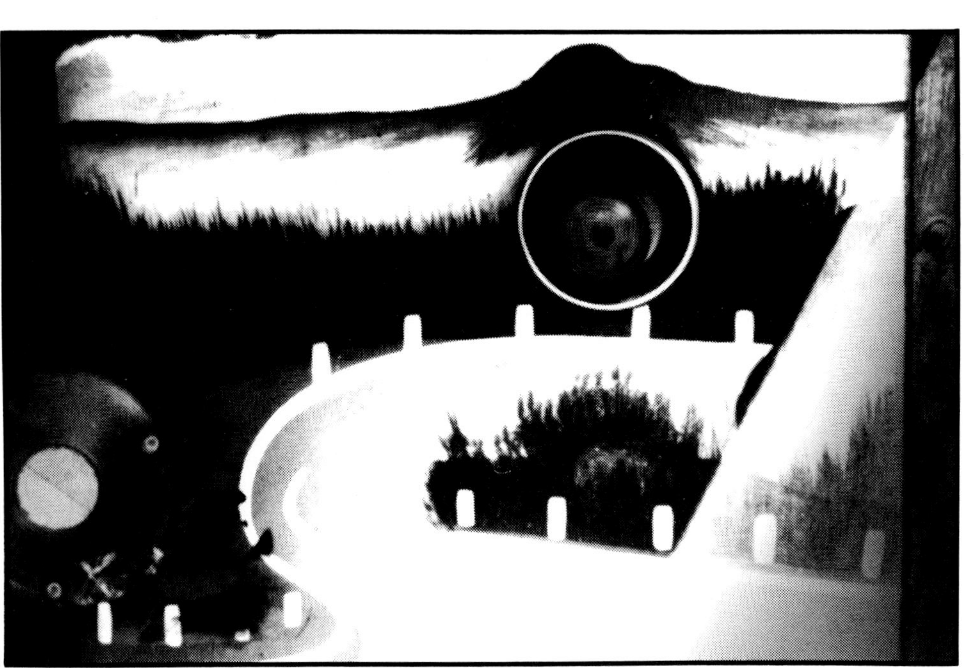

Puebla: No dicho, just an elaborate mudflap painting of a highway. It is not uncommon to see the name of a company, advertisements, or the ever-present SIGA—ALTO pair painted or stamped on a pair of mudflaps. 'Art' is less common and this is a good example of it. (MFT)

INTRODUCCIÓN

El dicho es un relato, una parte de una tradición 'hablada,' y así no se puede traducir prontamente en un diccionario. Las letras de estos dichos estan escritas muchas veces foneticamente, sin una silenciosa como H o con las letras cambiadas:

  B por V / C for Q / C por K / F por V / G por H / J por G / LL por Y / S por C y viceversa!

Dado la frecuencia de la ortografía incorrecta, la libertad gramática, y hecho que el autor de este libro no tiene la familiaridad del 'caló' de todos los países, la tarea de la traducción ha sido difícil.

No pude llegar a una traducción sólida para los "dichos" en este capítulo. ¿Cual la intención del pintor vehícular? Estos dichos misteriosos persistentes han sido incluídos por tres razones: primero, porque alguna alma apasionada hizo la molestia para pintarlos sobre su vehículo; siguiente, porque son atormentados; y, al fin, porque algún lector pueda saber el sentido o tal vez tenga buenas ideas de lo que sea la traducción.

BOLIVIA

LA PAZ
Rober / ? (short for Roberto?) *(SFT)*
Korilazo / ? (unknown) *(MFT)*

ECUADOR

QUITO
El Entrevido
(My taxidriver, Hugo Herrera, didn't know this one, either) *(SFT)*

GUATEMALA

GUATEMALA
Aúnque Me Odias Te Ceguire Quieriendo
Even Though You Hate Me, I Have Gone on Loving You.
(assumes seguiré and queriendo were intended) (LFT)

Has Nacido Libre – El Arrhadas / You Were Born Free / ? *(front, pickup truck)*
(If this were intended to be the word arracadas, *then the translation could be 'the hangers-on,'*
drawn from the expression for children who hang around a widow; contrasts with front of truck.
It could also be from arriadas, *and mean 'lazy ladies.')*

Yá Vinó Por Quién Morabas / ? Here Came the One You've Been Living For
or, Living (here) For. (Probably from morar which means live in the sense of dwell, but
could have been intended to be mirabas: Here I am, the One You've Been Looking For) *(MFT)*

GAVITA – CELOSA / ? Good for nothing – Jealous
(Assumes gaita was intended to match celosa; the next best possibility is gavia,
miner's slang for the 'madman's cage') (both words on each mudflap) (MFT)

Cíudad Juárez: "Banarru" – Chury / ? – Chury
An old, hard-used pickup truck doing business on both sides of the border between
El Paso, Texas, and Cíudad Juárez, Mexico.

La Paz: Rober (SFT)

QUETZALTENANGO
Precaución O.C. / Precaution, O.C. (What is meant by the initials O.C.?) (Bus)

MEXICO

ACAPULCO
Abelote / ? Acorn, (from abellotado; or abela, a black poplar; or bellote, a round-headed nail)
(MFT)

BERMEJILLO
Charflán / ? (Appeared on an 18-wheel logging truck with no hint as to the meaning)

CHILPANCINGO
Guita Verde / Green Thread or Green Money
(guita also means jealous, or treacherous, especially handling mules) (MFT)

CIUDAD JUÁREZ
Trabajo Poco Pero Para Frijoles Saco – Idonso
I Work (Just a) Little for Only a Sack of Beans – It is proper
(Assumes Idonso is misspelled and Idoneo intended) (hard-used MFT)

Gambusino / ? (The spelling is correctly transcribed, but the meaning is obscure.
In street slang, however, it can mean adventurer) (LFT)

CRUZ DE HUANACÁXTLE
Avispion Verde / ? (The meaning of this dicho is obscure.
If -pion means very pious, then the whole dicho could mean 'A Very Pious Green Bird.'
The Avispillo is a fragile tree from Puerto Rico) (MFT)

HUAJUAPAN DE LEÓN
Quirito Veneno / ? (Quirito may be from querido, a beloved; or quirite, a knight; and
veneno, poison, fury or passion, or, in street slang, strong whiskey: Beloved Drunk or
Passionate Drunkard? Quiquirito also means 'show-off) (MFT)

IGUALA

La Fargopeta / ? (Possibly from Pargo, Porgy, fish, and peta, please: Pleasing Porgy. I have
also seen this dicho twice on the back of 'FARGO' pickup trucks as La FARGO peta.) *(18-T)*

Chirris / The Creaker? (from Chirriar?) *(18-T)*

Cucho René / Snub-nosed Renee (from cucho, also meaning manure-compost;
or coche, car) *(LFT)*

MOROLEÓN

Cupando / ? (The meaning is not known, though cupana, in slang, is a healing drink
from a tree native to the Amazon) *(LFT)*

OAXACA

Papasquaro / ? (possibly from papa; or papas, lies; and papasal, and Pátzcuaro:
Playful Papa (Liar) from Pátzcuaro) *(LFT)*

La Banda del Carro Rojo / El Flaco / The Band of the Red Card – The Thin One
(or other possible translations. The true meaning is not known) *(MFT)*

Murmuren Viboras …que el Vabo Yo Soy Feliz
Vipers (women) are Gossiping…and, as the Vagabond, I Am Happy.
(Assumes vago or vado, though the intention is still not clear) *(SFT)*

Soñador Mucionado – Virgo 2^{0}_{ii}
? Lot-of-Nothing Dreamer – Virgo 2°/ii
Soñador is dreamer. Mucionado is very uncertain. Translation here assumes Mucio is a form of
Mucho with (de) Nada replacing nado. What is certain is that the dicho was on a large,
fruit-carrying farm truck)

El Manantial – Indayalu – Latetzi – Latuvi / The Spring – ?-?-?
(This PT was parked in the Oaxaca Market, but its owner could not be found.
Three untranslatable words may well be in Indian dialect)

PUEBLA

El Phagrote / ? (possibly a play on pagarote, the big spender; or from fregote, a macho;
or padrote, pimp; or pagote, one who gets another's blame) *(LFT)*

QUERÉTARO

El Ponchoreartos / ? (the meaning of this dicho is completely obscure) *(MFT)*

SAN JUAN DE LA PAZ

Raza Pero / ? (There are several meanings of each word. Possible translations:
Of the Race, but…; Defective Material; Faulty Race (Man); if puro intended, Pure Race) *(MFT)*

SAN LUÍS POTOSÍ

Picholco / ? (could be picholeo misspelled, and thus mean 'merry-making,' or 'business of
little account or worth') *(LFT)*

TAXCO
Jumilero / Flor Morena / Jumilero – Dark Flower
(Jumilero is not clear: if from jumíl, it suggests a real Mexican, one who eats toasted jumiles,
insects which sell for 5 pesos each; jumilero may also mean a 'Tascanian') *(MFT)*

TUXTLA GUTIERREZ
Mi Tegueño / ? (If from tegual, 'My Tax Burden'; if from tegue, then grower of tegue,
a tuberous plant of Venezuela; meaning obscure) *(18-T)*

YAÚTEPEC
El Teporocho / ? (Spelling uncertain because of the crude lettering.
If from táporo, one eyed, pig-headed, intelligent; if from taparazo, violent blow; from
taparero, gossip, story; if from toporo, a calabash cup. Lots of choices from street slang) *(MFT)*

PANAMA

PANAMÁ
Ajitando – Comparame / ? – Compare Me! (Ajitando is probably from Ahitando,
giving full satisfaction. It doesn't appear likely to be related to Aji, spicy, but who knows?)

No Quiero Maseo / I Don't Like ? ? (completely obscure) *(Bus)*

Viejito pero Cachimón / He's Old but He Can Shake those Dice!
(Assumes cachimona, abbreviated and strengthened by the ending -ón) *(Bus)*

Mi Sangre Atrévete / I Dare You!
(Sangre may stand here for courage, daring someone to cross in front of the Bus)

BIBLIOGRAFIA

Oaxaca: "Soy Tu Leño" / I Am Your Vessel (SFT)

Dichos, Dicharachos y Refranes Mexicanos. Editores Mexicanos Unidos, SA: Mexico DF, Mexico, 1977.

Edmonson, Munro S. *The Mexican Truck Driver,* chapter entitled "Contemporary Latin-American Culture." Publication 25, Middle American Research Institute, Tulane University: New Orleans, pp. 73-78, 1959.

Folino, Norberto, e Hijo. *Chofer Buena Banana Busca Chica Buena Mandarina.* Ediciones de la Flor, SRL: Buenos Aires, Argentina, 1974.

Franz, Carl. *The People's Guide to Mexico.* John Muir Publications: Santa Fe, 1979.

Giffords, Gloria Fraser. "Soul of the Mexican Trucker." *El Palacio, 87* No. 1, pp. 3-17, 1981.

Jaquith, James R. "Cawboy de Medianoche – Mexican Highway Folklore." *The New Scholar,* Vol. 5, No. 1, pp. 39-72, 1975.

Jiménez, A. *Picardía Mexicana.* Editores Mexicanos Unidos, L. González Obregón 5-B: México 1 DF, México, 1981.

Schmit, Marilee. *De Mi Te Olvidarás pero de lo Que Hisimos Jamas.* Thesis, Department of Anthropology, University of New Mexico: Albuquerque (Unpublished).

Woodward, Arthur. "Names On Wheels." *Westways Magazine,* Vol. 48, p. 34, November 1956.

DICCIONARIOS Y TEXTOS
DICTIONARIES & TEXTBOOKS

Americanismos: Diccionario Ilustrado Sopena. Editorial Ramón Sopena, SA: Provenza, 95, Barcelona, Spain, 1983.

Aranda, Charles. *Dichos.* Sunstone Press: Santa Fe, NM, 1977.

Ballesteros, Octavio A. *Mexican Proverbs: The Philosophy, Wisdom, and Humor of a People.* Eakin Press: Brunet, TX, 1979.

Barker, George Carpenter. *Pachuco.* University of Arizona Press: Tucson, AZ, 1970.

Campos, Juana G., and Ana Barella. *Diccionario de Refranes.* Anejos del Boletín de la Reál Academia Española: Madrid, 1975

Castelo, Hernán Rodríguez. *Lexico Sexuál Ecuatoriano y Latinoamericano.* Ediciones Libri Mundi, Instituto Otaveleño de Antropologia: Quito, Ecuador, 1979.

Cobos, Rubén. *Southwestern Spanish Proverbs.* San Marcos Press: Cerrillos, NM, 1974.

Combet, Louis. *Vocabulário de Refranes y Frases Proverbiales.* Institut d'Études Íberiques y Íbero-américaines de l'Université de Bordeaux: France, 1967.

Connelly, Tomás, y Tomás Higgins. *Diccionário Nuevo y Completo de las Lenguas Española e Inglesa.* Impresa Reál: Madrid, 1797.

Cuyás, Arturo. *Nuevo Diccionario Cuyas de Appleton.* Appleton-Century-Crofts: New York, 1966.

Diccionario Español-Inglés, Inglés-Español. The University of Chicago. Pocket Books: New York, NY, 1975.

Diccionário Politécnica de las Lenguas Española e Inglesa. Ed.: Castilla: Madrid, 1965.

Duarte, Feliz Rámos I. *Diccionário de Mejicanismos.* Impresa de E. Dublán: Mexico, 1895.

Fuentes, Dagoberto, and José A. López. *Barrio Language Dictionary.* El Barrio Publications: La Puente, CA, 1974.

Galván, Roberto A., and Richard V. Teschner. *El Diccionário del Español Chicano* Institute of Modern Languages: Silver Spring, MD, 1977.

Gámez, Tana de, Editor-in-Chief. *International Dictionary, English-Spanish, Spanish-English.* Simon and Schuster: New York, 1973.

García de Riverá, Clorinda. *Folklore Neomexicano.* Starline Printing: Albuquerque, NM, 1982.

Giraud, A. Frías-Sucre. *Diccionário Comerciál Español-Inglés, Inglés-Español; El Secretario.* Ed. Juventud: Barcelona, 1965.

Guerrero, Antonio Perol. *Nuevo Diccionario Técnico-Comercial.* Chemical Publishing Company: Brooklyn, NY, 1942.

Hernández-Chavez, Eduardo, Andrew D. Cohen, and Anthony F. Beltramo, eds. *El Lenguaje de los Chicanos.* Center for Applied Linguistics: Arlington, VA, 1975.

Klein, Esteban. *Rellenos para Uso Diário.* Editorial Rayuela: Buenos Aires, 1974.

Kloe, Donald R. *Un Diccionário Bilingue de las Exclamaciones e Interjecciones en Español e Inglés.* Ed. Universal: Miami, FL, 1976.

Paredes-Candia, Antonio. *Refranes, Frases y Expresiones Populares de Bolívia.* Ediciones Isla: La Paz, 1976.

Peers, Edgar A., et al., eds. *Cassell's Spanish Dictionary.* Funk and Wagnalls: New York, 1968.

Pérez, José. *Provérbios Brasileiros.* Ediçoes de Ouro: Rio de Janeiro, 1969.

Pinzón, Carlos Ernesto. *Dichos y Refranes Oídos en Colombia.* Instituto Colombiano de Cultura: Bogotá, 1973.

Rosensweig, Jay B. *Caló: Gutter Spanish.* Dutton: New York, 1973.

Storz, George C. *Mexican Spanish.* Commercial Press: San Diego, CA, 1945.

Tavera, José Maria. *El Refranero Popular Español.* Editorial de Gassó Hermanos: Madrid, 1977.

Torrents dels Prats, A. *Diccionario de Modismos, Inglés y Norte-Americano.* Editorial Juventud, SA: Barcelona, Spain, 1969.

Vasquez, Dr. Librado Keno, and Maria Enriqueta Vasquez. *Regional Dictionary of Chicano Slang.* Jenkins Publishing Company, Pemberton Press: Austin, TX, 1975.

Velásquez de la Cadena, Mariano, Edward Gray, and Juan L. Iribas. *The Revised Velásquez Spanish-English, English-Spanish Dictionary.* Prentice-Hall, Inc.: Englewood Cliffs, NJ, 1973.

Weiman, Ralph W., and O.A. Succar. *Common Usage Dictionary: Spanish-English English-Spanish.* Crown Publishers: New York, 1956.

Williams, Edwin B. *Diccionario Inglés-Español, Español-Inglés.* Bantam Books, Inc.: New York, NY, 1968.

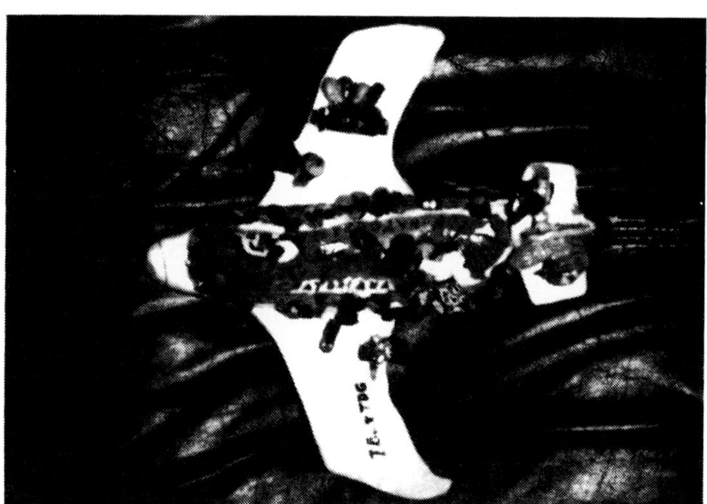

Quito: TBC Y TDG – Ecuatoriana / I Kissed You and I left You!
Presumably the method of travel was by Ecuatoriana Airlines! This small ceramic toy airplane was made available to me by Jill and John Ortman, the owners of La Bodega, from their private collection.